Tokenization of Trust

How Web3 is Redefining the Value of Digital Engagement

Joe Sticca

Technics Publications
SEDONA, ARIZONA

115 Linda Vista, Sedona, AZ 86336 USA
https://www.TechnicsPub.com

Edited by Jamie Hoberman
Cover design by Lorena Molinari

First Printing 2025

Copyright © 2025 by Joe Sticca

ISBN, print ed.   9781634626323
ISBN, Kindle ed.   9781634626330
ISBN, PDF ed.   9781634626347

Library of Congress Control Number: 2024952371

Contents

Chapter 1: The Web's Next Chapter: Decentralization & the Rise of Web3 1

The Role of Cooperative Structures in Web3 _____ 3

Governance in Web3_____ 3

Early Success: Why DAOs Initially Thrived _____ 4

Data Collection and Privacy in Web3 _____ 5

Chapter 2: The Core Technologies of Web3 _____ 7

Blockchain and Distributed Ledgers _____ 8

Cryptography and Decentralization _____ 9

Public and Private Keys_____10

Privacy and Data Ownership_____10

Smart Contracts _____11

Tokenization and Digital Assets _____13

Fungible Tokens _____13

Non-Fungible Tokens (NFTs)_____14

Tokenization _____15

Case Studies and Applications_____16

Redefining Data Ownership _____17

Chapter: 3: From Platforms to Protocols _____ 19

Decentralized Finance (DeFi) _____20

How Companies Are Engaging with DeFi_____20

DeFi in Action_____21

Why DeFi Matters to Companies _____22

Why DeFi is Critical for Financial Services _____23

Non-Fungible Tokens (NFTs)_____24

How Companies Are Using NFTs_____24

Examples of Corporate NFT Success_____25

Key Business Impacts of NFTs _____26

Expanding the NFT Use Case _____27

Decentralized Autonomous Organizations (DAOs) _____28

Empowering Communities _____28

Examples of DAOs in Action _____29

Key Business Impacts of DAO Adoption _____31

Challenges and Opportunities_____32

Layer 1 vs. Layer 2 Solutions _____33

Layer 1 Solutions (Base Blockchains) _____34

Layer 2 Solutions (Scalability Enhancements)_____35
Corporate Strategies Leveraging Layer 1 and Layer 2 Solutions _____36
Key Business Impacts of Layer 1 and Layer 2 Solutions _____37
Web3 and the Metaverse_____38
Corporate Strategy in the Metaverse_____38
Key Business Impacts of the Metaverse_____39
Additional Use Cases in the Metaverse_____41

Chapter 4: Leveraging Data for Profit in Web3 _____**43**
Revolutionizing Data with Web3 Applications_____44
NFTs as Engagement Tools_____44
Leveraging Decentralized Infrastructure for Competitive Advantage_____45
Turning a Liability into an Asset_____46
How Big Brands Are Winning in Web3 _____48
Making Data a Competitive Edge _____49

Chapter 5: The Convergence of AI_____**51**
AI in the Metaverse_____52
AI-Driven Personalization _____53
AI-Powered Economies _____54
Scaling Web3 with AI _____55
Transforming Digital Ownership with AI_____56
Winning in AI and Web3 Convergence _____57

Chapter 6: Digital Twins and AI Avatars _____**59**
Personalizing the User Experience _____60
Extending User Autonomy_____61
Fueling Immersive Digital Twins _____62
Ethical AI and User Privacy _____63
Monetizing AI in Virtual Worlds _____64
Ethical Oversight and Blockchain Security _____65
Big Companies, Big Wins in Web3_____66

Chapter 7: Decentralized Data, Centralized Profits _____**67**
Data Sovereignty_____68
Blockchain and Privacy-First Technologies _____69
Anonymity and Ownership_____70
Balancing Transparency and Privacy for Mass Adoption _____71
Privacy-Driven Revenue Models in the Web3 Metaverse _____72
Data Privacy as the Future of Digital Commerce _____73

Chapter 8: AI-Driven Smart Contracts and Governance _____ **75**

AI-Enhanced Smart Contracts _____76

Bridging On-Chain and Off-Chain Worlds_____77

AI in DAO Governance_____79

Corporate Gains from AI in Web3 _____80

Building the Future of Decentralized Business _____81

Chapter 9: Portable Identities, Profitable Futures _____ **83**

Data Portability in Web3_____84

Decentralized Identifiers (DIDs)_____85

Personal Data Stores _____85

Tokenized Data Ownership_____86

Monetizing Data Sovereignty _____87

The Competitive Advantage of Data Sovereignty _____87

Looking Ahead: A Decentralized Future_____88

Key Takeaways for Enterprises _____89

Chapter 10: Real-Time Data Analytics in the Metaverse _____ **91**

AI-Driven Real-Time Insights_____92

Predictive Analytics_____93

Real-Time Data as a Corporate Resource _____95

The Future of Big Business in the Metaverse_____96

Key Takeaways for Enterprises _____96

Chapter 11: Ethical AI and Responsible Data Management_____ **97**

Corporate Integration of Ethical AI in Decentralized Systems _____98

Tackling AI Bias in Web3 _____99

DAO-Led Ethical AI Standards_____101

The Business of Responsible Data Management _____102

Web3's Ethical AI Opportunity_____103

Chapter 12: Tokenized Data and the Virtual Economy _____ **105**

Tokenizing Data _____106

Revolutionizing Ownership and Representation_____107

Incentives for Data Sharing_____108

Turning Data into Digital Assets_____109

Building New Marketplaces _____110

Capitalizing on Web3's Tokenized Economy _____112

Chapter 13: The Interoperability Edge _____**113**
AI-Driven Cross-Chain Data Ecosystems _____114
Cross-Chain NFT and dApp Interactions _____115
AI-Driven Consistent User Experiences Across Web3 Platforms _____116
The Role of Decentralized Oracles Enhanced by AI _____117
AI-Enhanced Interoperability as a Growth Catalyst _____118
The Future of AI in Web3 Interoperability _____119
The Competitive Edge in AI-Powered Web3 _____119

Chapter 14: Data Monetization in Web3_____**121**
Reinventing Revenue Models _____122
AI-Driven Data Marketplaces _____123
Empowering Creators _____125
Turning Data and Creativity into Revenue _____126
Redefining the Digital Economy _____127

Index _____**129**

CHAPTER ONE

The Web's Next Chapter: Decentralization and the Rise of Web3

Web3, often called the "Ownership Economy," marks a new phase of the internet where users and builders, rather than centralized entities, hold control and value. Unlike Web2, which centralized data and influence within large tech companies, Web3 emphasizes decentralization, ownership, and data sovereignty.

To understand Web3, it helps to look back. **Web1** was about information-sharing—static pages that allowed for passive consumption. **Web2**, beginning in 2005, introduced an interactive web where social media platforms, apps, and other closed networks allowed anyone to connect and share. This era, known as the "Platform Economy," brought vast connectivity but also centralized power, as platforms like Facebook, Twitter, and Google controlled users' data and access to audiences.

In **Web3**, however, decentralization returns control to users. Built on blockchain or distributed ledger technology, Web3 platforms operate without intermediaries, allowing users to hold tokens representing ownership in a network or application. These tokens, whether fungible (cryptocurrencies) or non-fungible (NFTs), give users a real stake in the systems they use. Here, users have autonomy over their data, and the value generated in these networks stays with the community. This decentralization fundamentally shifts the model of value from platform-centered to user-centered, building a more equitable internet landscape.

Era	Monetization Strategies	Main Players
🌐 **Web 1.0** *(Early Internet)*	- Simple Advertisements - Sponsorships - Basic E-commerce	- Yahoo - AOL - Netscape - Amazon - eBay
🔗 **Web 3.0** *(Decentralized & User-Owned Web)*	- View-and-Earn Advertisements - Tokenization (crypto, NFTs) - Protocol Fees - Decentralized Paywalls & Subscriptions	- Ethereum - Uniswap - Aave - Brave - Mirror

The Role of Cooperative Structures in Web3

Web3's approach to community-based governance resembles the cooperative model, where all participants are vested in the organization's success. Cooperatives, or "co-ops," have long operated on a similar principle, where members contribute to and share in the outcomes of the organization. In Web3, this concept takes form through **Decentralized Autonomous Organizations (DAOs)**. Like co-ops, DAOs distribute governance to members, creating an organization that is transparent, democratic, and user-owned.

In a Web3 setting, DAOs allow users to vote on platform changes, allocate resources, and influence development decisions, all without a central authority. This model gives everyone "skin in the game," aligning incentives and ensuring that users are not merely consumers but active stakeholders.

Much like cooperatives, DAOs foster shared interests and collective success, creating a community-first approach that enhances user loyalty and drives innovation.

Governance in Web3

In 2021, Decentralized Autonomous Organizations (DAOs) experienced a surge in popularity, becoming a leading model for community-led governance in the Web3 ecosystem. DAOs presented a vision where users held governance power through token ownership, making decisions collectively without the need for traditional corporate intermediaries. However, as of 2023, the DAO landscape has shifted significantly. The enthusiasm that fueled the initial boom has waned, with declining participation, reduced funding, and numerous operational challenges leading many DAOs to either evolve or dissolve. This section explores the trajectory of DAOs, analyzing both their early successes and the emerging obstacles that threaten their future.

Early Success: Why DAOs Initially Thrived

DAOs initially captivated the crypto community by offering an innovative approach to governance based on transparency, community ownership, and decentralized decision-making. A classic example is **The DAO** from 2016, which raised over $150 million in ETH, capturing around 15% of all ETH at the time. This crowdfunded project allowed token holders to vote on proposals and receive potential returns if funded projects succeeded. Such decentralized, transparent structures empowered communities to collectively fund initiatives, set policies, and govern resources, contrasting sharply with the closed decision-making of traditional corporations.

Another early success story, **MakerDAO**, introduced a stablecoin system where members voted on collateral types and risk parameters. Similarly, **Uniswap DAO** allowed participants to decide on protocol upgrades and treasury management, illustrating how community-driven decisions could directly impact high-value DeFi applications. These DAOs represented a revolutionary approach to governance, supported by token-based voting mechanisms and blockchain transparency.

Data Collection and Privacy in Web3

One of the most transformative shifts in Web3 is its redefined approach to data collection and privacy, addressing many of the issues associated with Web2. In Web2, platforms such as Facebook, Google, and Twitter(now X) rely heavily on data monetization, generating **billions in ad revenue** by selling user information to advertisers. This centralized model has raised significant privacy concerns, with **91% of U.S. adults** reporting they feel they have "lost control" over how their personal information is collected and used by companies.[1] Users have little to no say in how their data is accessed, shared, or monetized, creating a lack of transparency and control.

In contrast, Web3 champions data sovereignty by putting users in control of their personal information. Through blockchain's decentralized structure, data in Web3 is stored across distributed

---

[1] https://www.pewresearch.org/short-reads/2018/03/27/americans-complicated-feelings-about-social-media-in-an-era-of-privacy-concerns/

networks rather than on centralized servers, reducing the risk of data breaches and unauthorized access. This distributed setup also increases transparency, as users can verify data integrity and access permissions without relying on a central authority.

Web3 also introduces advanced privacy-focused tools like Zero-Knowledge Proofs (ZKPs), a cryptographic method that allows data verification without exposing the actual information. ZKPs are gaining popularity, with platforms like zkSync and Aztec using these proofs to protect user identities, ensuring that transactions can be verified while keeping personal details private. By 2024, the adoption of ZKPs has grown significantly, with estimates suggesting a **25% year-on-year increase** in applications using this technology to enhance privacy.

Web3's model fundamentally reimagines data privacy by moving away from Web2's data extraction model to one where users retain control and ownership of their digital footprint. This shift towards individual data autonomy empowers users to decide how, when, and with whom to share their information, laying the foundation for a more transparent, privacy-respecting internet.

CHAPTER TWO

The Core Technologies of Web3

Web3 represents a radical departure from the traditional internet model, shifting control from centralized entities to a decentralized, user-owned framework. This chapter explores the core technologies that form the backbone of Web3, each contributing to a more open, trustless, and self-governing digital environment. These key technologies include blockchain and distributed ledgers, cryptography, smart contracts, and tokenization, all of which enable users to own and control their digital assets and interactions directly, without intermediaries.

Blockchain and Distributed Ledgers

Blockchain technology, the core infrastructure of Web3, enables a decentralized and trustless environment where data is managed across a distributed network rather than a centralized authority. According to 2023 data, the global blockchain market size is projected to reach over $39 billion by 2025, growing at an annual rate of over 67%. This explosive growth highlights blockchain's role as the backbone of Web3, supporting applications that prioritize security, transparency, and trust.[2]

In Web3, blockchain's open ledger system ensures data immutability and transparency. A 2022 report by Chainalysis found that blockchain's immutability has been crucial for industries needing secure records, such as finance and healthcare. Transactions recorded on blockchain cannot be altered without achieving network consensus, a quality that prevents tampering and builds trust among users. Blockchain's decentralized structure eliminates the need for traditional intermediaries, placing data ownership and control directly into the hands of users. Unlike Web2, where tech giants control data and user interactions, Web3 platforms operate on blockchain protocols that distribute

---

[2] https://www.prnewswire.com/news-releases/the-global-blockchain-market-size-is-expected-to-grow-from-usd-3-0-billion-in-2020-to-usd-39-7-billion-by-2025--at-a-compound-annual-growth-rate-cagr-of-67-3-301058443.html#:~:text=%2F%3Futm_source%3DPRN-,The%20global%20blockchain%20market%20size%20is%20expected%20to%20grow%20from,67.3%25%20during%20the%20forecast%20period

ownership. For instance, Ethereum, the leading Web3 platform, has over 400,000 active developers as of 2023, reflecting strong user participation in governance and platform evolution. This shift towards user-centric control is further supported by token economies within these networks; Ethereum alone has a market capitalization exceeding $200 billion, demonstrating the value placed on user-governed ecosystems.[3]

Each blockchain network operates with its own protocol and issues tokens representing both value and governance rights. On platforms like Polkadot and Cosmos, token holders participate in key decisions, from technical upgrades to resource allocation.

Cryptography and Decentralization

Cryptography is the backbone of security and decentralization in Web3, creating a secure environment for interactions and transactions without relying on a central authority.

In the Web3 ecosystem, cryptographic techniques are essential for safeguarding transactions, protecting user identities, and ensuring data integrity—allowing users to interact and transact in a trustless environment.

---

[3] https://www.statista.com/statistics/807195/ethereum-market-capitalization-quarterly/

Public and Private Keys

Central to Web3 security is the use of public and private key cryptography, a system that enables users to control access to their digital assets and data. Public keys act as addresses to which anyone can send information, while private keys serve as passwords that allow only the rightful owner to access or authorize transactions. This cryptographic mechanism underpins the security of over $100 billion in digital assets on blockchains like Ethereum and Bitcoin, allowing users to securely manage and transact without intermediaries.

Privacy and Data Ownership

One of Web3's defining characteristics is its emphasis on user-controlled privacy. In traditional Web2 platforms, user data is typically owned and controlled by centralized companies, who can often access, share, or monetize it without user consent. In contrast, Web3 cryptography empowers users with true ownership of their digital identities, allowing them to selectively share data. For instance, according to a 2023 survey by ConsenSys, 83% of Web3 users cite privacy as a primary reason for adopting decentralized applications, with cryptographic protections ensuring that users can control who accesses their data.[4]

Smart Contracts

Smart contracts are self-executing agreements written directly into blockchain code, enabling automated transactions without the need for intermediaries. These contracts operate on the "code is law" principle: the contract terms are defined in code and executed automatically when predefined conditions are met. Ethereum, the second-largest blockchain by market cap, pioneered the use of smart contracts, accounting for approximately 57% of all decentralized applications (dApps) in 2023, according to DappRadar.[5]

One of the primary uses of smart contracts is managing and transferring ownership of digital assets, including fungible tokens and non-fungible tokens (NFTs). With ownership rules encoded in smart contracts, digital assets such as artwork, music, or videos can be transferred directly between users in a secure, transparent manner. Smart contracts also enable creators to receive royalties automatically on secondary sales, ensuring a continued revenue

---

[4] https://consensys.io/insight-report/web3-and-crypto-global-survey-2023

[5] https://dappradar.com/blog/dapp-industry-report-2023-defi-nft-web3-games

stream—an innovation that has generated millions for BAYC (Bored Ape Yacht Club) and other popular collections.

Beyond digital collectibles, smart contracts extend to real-world applications. Data from Chainlink shows that NFTs and smart contracts are increasingly being used as collateral in decentralized finance (DeFi), with the NFT lending market surpassing $2 billion in 2024.[6] Real estate, legal documents, and high-value assets can also be represented as NFTs, enabling fractional ownership and secure, blockchain-based transactions. For example, companies like Propy use smart contracts to facilitate real estate sales, streamlining transactions by eliminating traditional intermediaries and providing verifiable, immutable records on the blockchain.

Through their ability to automate, verify, and enforce agreements, smart contracts are transforming industries beyond digital art, including finance, property, and intellectual property management.

Their transparency, security, and programmability are redefining asset ownership and transaction mechanisms in Web3, illustrating the immense potential of this technology in a decentralized digital economy.

---

[6] https://cryptobriefing.com/blend-nft-lending-growth/

Tokenization and Digital Assets

Tokenization has become a fundamental pillar of Web3, transforming how digital ownership and value are represented and managed. The market for tokenized digital assets is expanding rapidly, with data showing that the global tokenization market was valued at approximately $3.45 billion in 2024[7] and is projected to grow at a Compound Annual Growth Rate (CAGR) of 24% over the next decade. This surge is primarily driven by the use of both fungible tokens (FTs) and non-fungible tokens (NFTs), each of which enables unique forms of digital ownership.

Fungible Tokens

Fungible tokens, such as Bitcoin (BTC) and Ether (ETH), function as interchangeable units with equal value—akin to traditional currencies. These tokens facilitate secure, decentralized transactions and store values across blockchain networks. Their usage has grown exponentially. For instance, Bitcoin's daily transaction volume surpassed $10 billion in 2023, underscoring the demand for decentralized, borderless currency systems.[8]

---

[7] https://www.thebusinessresearchcompany.com/report/tokenization-global-market-report

[8] https://www.thecryptoalert.com/post/bitcoin-s-daily-trading-volume-surpasses-10-billion-pushing-btc-into-positive-territory-amid-bear

Fungible tokens also play an essential role in decentralized governance. In protocols like **Uniswap** and **Aave**, token holders can vote on critical decisions, such as protocol upgrades and treasury management.

Non-Fungible Tokens (NFTs)

NFTs, on the other hand, represent unique digital assets and are not interchangeable. They have revolutionized the ownership of digital content, enabling traceable, verifiable ownership of everything from artwork to virtual real estate. NFT market data from DappRadar highlights that in 2021 alone, the total sales volume for NFTs exceeded $25 billion, driven by high-profile transactions in digital art, music, and gaming. [9]By 2024, the market has become more diversified, with NFTs being used not only in art but also for assets in metaverse platforms, sports memorabilia, and utility-based applications.

Platforms like **OpenSea** and **Rarible** have become popular marketplaces for NFT transactions, collectively handling millions of dollars in daily trading volume. For example, OpenSea processed over $300 million in NFT transactions in January 2023,

---

[9] https://www.reuters.com/markets/europe/nft-sales-hit-25-billion-2021-growth-shows-signs-slowing-2022-01-10/

showcasing the growing demand for decentralized ownership models.[10]

Tokenization

Tokenization enables both fungible and non-fungible tokens to represent real value in digital form. In Web3, this transformation has implications across industries, from finance to entertainment. Unlike Web2, where assets and data are owned by centralized platforms, Web3 assets are controlled directly by the users. This shift is visible in the rapid adoption of DeFi (Decentralized Finance) protocols and NFT platforms, where ownership and participation are incentivized.

A survey by Deloitte shows that 80% of financial executives believe tokenization could fundamentally transform financial markets in the next five to ten years.[11] This confidence is supported by data indicating that the DeFi sector alone grew to over $800 billion in total locked value (TVL) in 2024, with tokenized assets being the

---

[10] https://www.musicbusinessworldwide.com/nft-marketplace-openseas-trading-volume-nosedives-99-is-the-bubble-bursting/

[11] https://www2.deloitte.com/content/dam/insights/articles/US144337_Blockchain-survey/DI_Blockchain-survey.pdf

primary driver.[12] Tokenization allows users to invest in, trade, and hold digital assets with transparent ownership and accountability, incentivizing engagement by giving users "skin in the game."

Case Studies and Applications

- **Real Estate and Tokenization**: Platforms like **RealT** enable fractional ownership of real estate via tokenization, allowing investors to own shares of properties represented by tokens. According to RealT, some properties have attracted over 1,000 unique investors, with token prices reflecting real-world asset appreciation.

- **Gaming and In-Game Assets**: In the gaming sector, tokenized assets are becoming prevalent, with games like **Axie Infinity** generating over $1 billion in NFT sales in 2021 alone.[13] Players buy, trade, and earn tokens by participating in in-game economies, providing them with true ownership of their digital assets.

- **Art and Cultural Preservation**: In the art world, NFTs enable artists to directly monetize their work. The sale of

---

[12] https://medium.com/coinmonks/defi-market-surges-as-total-value-locked-tvl-surpasses-80-billion-milestone-f4880a06d6a0

[13] https://forkast.news/nft-game-axie-infinity-revenue-2021/

Beeple's "Everydays: The First 5000 Days" NFT for $69 million in 2021 demonstrated the high value attributed to digital art when ownership is secured through blockchain.[14]

Redefining Data Ownership

Blockchain, cryptography, smart contracts, and tokenization form the foundational technologies of Web3, collectively enabling a decentralized, user-centered internet. Through these tools, Web3 platforms redefine ownership, allowing individuals to control

---

[14] https://www.theverge.com/2021/3/11/22325054/beeple-christies-nft-sale-cost-everydays-69-million

their data, manage digital assets, and participate in the governance of the platforms they use. Web3, therefore, marks a transformative shift toward a digital landscape where value is shared by the community rather than concentrated among a few centralized entities. This ownership economy sets the stage for a more inclusive and equitable internet, where everyone benefits from the value they help to create.

CHAPTER THREE

From Platforms to Protocols

The transition from Web2 to Web3 is not just an evolution of technology—it's a fundamental restructuring of the internet as we know it. Web3 prioritizes decentralization, transparency, and user ownership, creating opportunities for companies to innovate and dominate new markets. While Web2 giants like Facebook and Google centralized control over user data and experiences, the Web3 era empowers users to own their assets and data. Companies entering this space leverage the Web3 ecosystem to unlock new business models, enhance user engagement, and redefine value creation.

Let's explore how big players are capitalizing on the core elements of Web3—DeFi, NFTs, DAOs, Layer 1 and Layer 2 solutions, and the metaverse.

Decentralized Finance (DeFi)

DeFi represents a seismic shift in the financial services industry, challenging traditional banking systems and opening new opportunities for innovation. By leveraging blockchain-based peer-to-peer (P2P) protocols, DeFi eliminates the need for intermediaries like banks, brokers, and clearinghouses. This creates a direct, transparent, and automated financial ecosystem where transactions are faster, costs are lower, and accessibility is global. Here's how big companies are actively leveraging DeFi and its transformative potential.

How Companies Are Engaging with DeFi

- **Building Proprietary Platforms:** Companies like JPMorgan are investing heavily in building their own blockchain-based DeFi platforms. JPMorgan's Onyx platform, for example, provides a settlement system for institutional clients, using blockchain technology to streamline transactions and reduce operational bottlenecks.

- **Integration with Existing Systems:** Established financial players such as Visa and Mastercard are exploring blockchain networks for integrating stablecoins (cryptocurrencies pegged to fiat currencies like the

USD). These efforts reduce friction in cross-border payments, cutting down transaction times from days to minutes.

- **Partnerships with DeFi Innovators:** Big companies are collaborating with DeFi startups to gain a foothold in this space. For instance, financial institutions may partner with decentralized lending platforms to provide blockchain-based financial services under their own brands.

- **Tokenization of Assets:** Firms are enabling the tokenization of physical and digital assets, allowing users to buy, sell, or trade fractional ownership on DeFi platforms. This strategy not only democratizes access to traditionally illiquid assets (like real estate or art) but also creates entirely new markets.

DeFi in Action

- Visa and Mastercard are piloting the use of stablecoins like USDC for global payment settlements. By integrating blockchain technology into their payment networks, they reduce reliance on traditional banking intermediaries, cutting transaction fees and enabling near-instant transfers.

Impact: A more efficient, borderless payment system that enhances their relevance in cryptocurrencies.

- JPMorgan's Onyx platform facilitates blockchain-based settlements for large-scale institutional transactions. The system enables faster settlements while reducing counterparty risks and back-office reconciliation.

Impact: Lower costs, improved efficiency, and a competitive edge in servicing high-volume clients.

- PayPal is integrating cryptocurrency buying, selling, and storage capabilities into its platform. It is also rumored to be exploring decentralized lending and staking options to offer new financial products to its users.

Impact: A broader portfolio of financial services and deeper engagement with the crypto-savvy audience.

Why DeFi Matters to Companies

DeFi introduces new income streams for companies, including:

- **Transaction Fees:** Companies can generate revenue by facilitating DeFi transactions on their platforms.

- **Lending and Borrowing Services:** Platforms earn through interest rates or fees on decentralized loans.

- **Asset Tokenization:** Fractional ownership of tokenized assets creates ongoing opportunities for monetization.

DeFi is inherently borderless, meaning companies can:

- Serve previously untapped markets, like the unbanked and underbanked populations in emerging economies.

- Expand their financial footprint without the need for traditional infrastructure, lowering barriers to entry in global markets.

Replacing traditional intermediaries with smart contracts offer:

- **Reduced Operational Overhead:** Automation through smart contracts eliminates the need for manual processes and back-office operations.

- **Increased Transparency:** Blockchain's immutable nature ensures transactions are transparent and auditable.

- **Lower Costs:** Cutting out middlemen reduces fees for both the company and its users.

Why DeFi is Critical for Financial Services

DeFi is not just a trend; it is a fundamental restructuring of financial services that aligns with the broader push toward decentralization. Companies that embrace DeFi early are positioning themselves at the forefront of this transformation, capturing market share in a rapidly evolving space. Whether it's through tokenized assets, decentralized lending, or blockchain-based payment systems, DeFi is creating opportunities for revenue growth, cost efficiency, and global scalability.

> *For corporations, the DeFi revolution is both a challenge and an opportunity. Those that adapt will not only thrive but also help shape the future of global finance.*

Non-Fungible Tokens (NFTs)

NFTs are transforming the way digital ownership is perceived and monetized, creating immense opportunities for businesses to innovate and grow. By certifying unique ownership of digital or physical assets using blockchain technology, NFTs have redefined customer interaction, engagement, and monetization strategies.

How Companies Are Using NFTs

Brands are leveraging NFTs to connect with their audiences in creative, meaningful ways, creating not just products but ecosystems. These strategies include:

- **Enhancing Customer Experiences:** NFTs serve as a bridge between the physical and digital realms, offering exclusive content, experiences, and privileges.

- **Building Virtual Economies:** By enabling users to buy, sell, and trade digital assets, brands foster vibrant, self-sustaining economies.

- **Monetizing Loyalty:** NFTs allow companies to reward loyal customers and fans with unique, valuable items tied to their brand.

Examples of Corporate NFT Success

- Nike acquired RTFKT Studios to produce NFT sneakers for virtual worlds. Users can purchase, collect, and even show off their digital sneakers in the metaverse.

  Impact: This move positions Nike as a leader in the virtual goods space, driving engagement among tech-savvy, younger audiences who are invested in metaverse experiences.

- WMG partnered with NFT platforms to release exclusive music, virtual merchandise, and digital concert experiences. Fans can own a piece of their favorite artists' work or gain VIP access to events.

Impact: WMG deepens fan-artist connections while unlocking new revenue through direct-to-fan sales and secondary royalties from NFT resales.

- Gucci, Louis Vuitton, and others launched NFT collections, enabling customers to own digital versions of high-end fashion items for use in virtual environments like Decentraland or Roblox.

Impact: This initiative reinforces their luxury status, attracts a new demographic of tech-focused consumers, and opens up a hybrid market for physical-digital (phygital) goods.

Key Business Impacts of NFTs

- **Customer Loyalty and Engagement:** NFTs provide a way to reward customers with exclusive content or privileges. For example, owning a brand's NFT might grant access to special events, early product drops, or VIP memberships.

Result: These personalized rewards strengthen emotional ties to the brand, enhancing customer lifetime value.

- **New Revenue Streams:** Brands earn not only from the initial NFT sale but also from royalties when NFTs are resold on secondary markets. Smart contracts automate these royalty payments, ensuring consistent income over time.

Result: Recurring revenue transforms static sales into dynamic, long-term financial opportunities.

- **Cross-Platform Portability:** Unlike traditional assets confined to a single platform, NFTs are built on interoperable blockchain standards. This allows users to take their digital assets (e.g., virtual sneakers or gaming items) across different games, platforms, or metaverses.

Result: This flexibility enhances the value of the NFT and builds customer trust in its long-term utility.

Expanding the NFT Use Case

Beyond the examples above, brands are exploring the following:

- **Gaming:** Epic Games and Ubisoft are integrating NFTs into their games, allowing players to own, trade, and monetize in-game assets.

- **Real Estate:** Platforms like Propy are using NFTs to represent ownership of physical properties, simplifying property transactions.

- **Event Ticketing:** NFT tickets for concerts or sports events ensure secure, traceable, and fraud-proof entry, while also offering collectible value.

- **Phygital Products:** Brands combine physical goods (e.g., a designer handbag) with digital twins as NFTs, creating an enhanced ownership experience.

Decentralized Autonomous Organizations (DAOs)

Decentralized Autonomous Organizations (DAOs) are emerging as transformative governance models in the Web3 landscape, shifting decision-making power from centralized hierarchies to communities of stakeholders. Companies that integrate DAO principles are not only enhancing transparency and trust but also building strong, engaged user communities that feel a sense of ownership in the platform's success. Here's a deeper dive into the corporate strategies, examples, and key impacts of DAOs in business.

Empowering Communities

Traditional organizations often operate with centralized leadership, where decision-making is confined to a small group of executives or shareholders. In contrast, DAOs democratize governance by leveraging blockchain technology and token-based incentives. Companies adopt DAO structures to:

- **Involve Users in Governance:** Token holders vote on key decisions, such as product development, platform upgrades, and financial allocations.

- **Enhance Community Loyalty:** By giving users a stake in the organization's future, DAOs foster long-term commitment.

- **Decentralize Operations:** Smart contracts automate tasks, reducing reliance on centralized management and increasing efficiency.

DAOs align the interests of the organization with its community, creating a symbiotic relationship where all stakeholders benefit from the platform's growth and success.

Examples of DAOs in Action

- **Uniswap:** A leading decentralized exchange (DEX), Uniswap operates under a DAO governance model. Token holders (via the UNI token) propose and vote on changes to the platform, including feature development, fee structures, and partnerships.

Impact: This model ensures that the platform evolves in a way that benefits its community of users and liquidity providers, rather than solely focusing on corporate profits.

- **Andreessen Horowitz (a16z):** The venture capital giant has been actively investing in DAO-based projects. By supporting DAOs, a16z is fostering innovation in decentralized governance, particularly in areas like funding open-source software or managing community-driven projects.

  Impact: These initiatives are accelerating the adoption of DAO models across industries, proving their viability as an alternative to traditional governance structures.

- **MakerDAO:** MakerDAO is a decentralized lending platform where governance is driven by holders of the MKR token. Members vote on critical decisions, such as adjustments to the protocol's stability fee or collateral types.

  Impact: MakerDAO showcases how decentralized governance can effectively manage complex financial systems, inspiring other industries to explore DAO models.

Key Business Impacts of DAO Adoption

- **Community Ownership:** Companies distribute governance tokens to users, partners, or employees, granting them voting rights on key decisions. For example, a platform might allocate tokens based on user activity, rewarding loyal contributors.

  Business Benefit: This structure creates a sense of ownership among users, motivating them to advocate for and actively participate in the platform's success.

- **Transparency:** All governance proposals, votes, and financial transactions are recorded on the blockchain, making them publicly accessible.

  Business Benefit: Transparency builds trust, especially in industries where opaque decision-making has traditionally eroded confidence (e.g., finance, social media, or healthcare).

- **Reduced Administrative Costs:** Smart contracts automate repetitive or complex governance processes, such as executing payouts or enforcing voting results.

  Business Benefit: Automation reduces the need for human oversight, lowering operational costs and minimizing the risk of errors or corruption.

- **Rapid Decision-Making:** DAOs can enable faster decision-making by crowdsourcing opinions and executing pre-set conditions through smart contracts. This eliminates lengthy approval chains typical of centralized organizations.

  Business Benefit: Companies can remain agile, quickly responding to market shifts or user feedback.

- **Global Inclusivity:** DAOs are inherently borderless, allowing anyone with an internet connection and the required tokens to participate in governance.

  Business Benefit: This inclusivity attracts a diverse set of contributors, enriching decision-making with perspectives from around the world.

Challenges and Opportunities

While DAOs offer immense potential, companies must also address certain challenges to ensure their successful implementation:

Challenges:

- **Complexity:** Building and maintaining smart contracts require technical expertise and errors in code can have significant repercussions.

- **Coordination:** Achieving consensus among large, decentralized communities can be slow and contentious.

- **Regulation:** DAOs operate in legal grey areas in many jurisdictions, raising questions about liability, compliance, and taxation.

Opportunities:

- **Brand Differentiation:** Adopting a DAO structure positions companies as innovators, appealing to tech-savvy users and investors.

- **Community Growth:** DAOs attract users who value transparency and inclusion, fostering organic growth.

- **Cross-Industry Applications:** Beyond tech and finance, DAOs are being explored in areas like real estate (fractional property ownership), entertainment (fan-driven content production), and non-profits (community-managed funds).

Layer 1 vs. Layer 2 Solutions

In the Web3 ecosystem, scalability is one of the most critical challenges and opportunities. As the adoption of blockchain technology grows, networks face bottlenecks in transaction speed, cost, and capacity. Layer 1 and Layer 2 solutions address these issues, enabling Web3 applications to scale efficiently, support massive user bases, and remain cost-effective. For businesses, investing in these solutions means positioning themselves as enablers and beneficiaries of a more robust and scalable decentralized internet.

Layer 1 Solutions (Base Blockchains)

Layer 1 refers to the foundational blockchains like Ethereum, Bitcoin, and Solana. These blockchains handle basic functionalities such as validating transactions, executing smart contracts, and maintaining decentralization. However, as activity increases, these networks often face congestion, leading to higher fees and slower transaction times.

Examples of Layer 1 Improvements include:

- **Ethereum 2.0 (The Merge):** Transitioning to a Proof-of-Stake (PoS) consensus mechanism to improve energy efficiency and scalability.

- **Sharding:** A method that divides the blockchain into smaller, manageable sections to process transactions in parallel.

- **Algorand and Solana:** Emerging Layer 1 blockchain offering faster transactions and lower fees natively.

Layer 2 Solutions (Scalability Enhancements)

Layer 2 solutions build on top of Layer 1 blockchains to improve performance without compromising security. These solutions process transactions off-chain or in secondary layers, reducing the workload on the main blockchain.

Examples of Layer 2 Technologies include:

- **Rollups (Optimistic and ZK-Rollups):** Bundle multiple transactions and settle them on the main chain as a single batch.

- **Polygon:** A Layer 2 network reducing costs and enabling fast transactions for Ethereum.

- **Arbitrum and Optimism:** Optimistic Rollups improving Ethereum scalability.

- **State Channels:** Off-chain channels for direct interactions between parties, later settling results on-chain.

- **Sidechains:** Independent blockchains connected to the main chain, such as xDai or Ronin, designed for specific use cases like gaming or payments.

Corporate Strategies Leveraging Layer 1 and 2 Solutions

- **Infrastructure as a Service, such as Microsoft and Google Cloud:** By offering blockchain-as-a-service (BaaS), these tech giants are enabling developers to deploy and manage blockchain applications seamlessly. This reduces the complexity of building on Layer 1 chains while encouraging mass adoption of blockchain technology.

- **Transaction Efficiency and User Experience, such as Coinbase and Binance:** These platforms are integrating Layer 2 solutions like Polygon to reduce transaction fees and improve processing speed. This enhances the user experience for activities like trading, DeFi participation, and NFT transactions.

- **Strategic Investments, such as Visa and PayPal:** Visa and PayPal are investing in Layer 1 and Layer 2 technologies to explore new payment systems that combine the security of Layer 1 with the efficiency of Layer 2.

Key Business Impacts of Layer 1 and 2 Solutions

- **Enhanced Scalability:** Scalability is essential for mass adoption. Layer 2 solutions significantly reduce congestion and transaction fees, enabling platforms to handle millions of users.

  Corporate Opportunity: Companies can build and host applications that support real-time interactions, from decentralized finance (DeFi) to gaming and beyond, without compromising on performance.

- **Market Expansion:** Lower fees and faster transactions attract more users, especially from emerging markets where transaction costs are prohibitive.

  Corporate Opportunity: Businesses can onboard a diverse user base, offering accessible solutions across industries such as gaming, e-commerce, and banking.

- **Interoperability:** Blockchain ecosystems must communicate seamlessly to ensure smooth user experiences and asset portability.

  Corporate Opportunity: Companies investing in interoperable solutions can act as bridges between blockchains, becoming central to the Web3 ecosystem and capturing value through fees or proprietary standards.

Web3 and the Metaverse

The metaverse is evolving into a transformative space where the digital and physical worlds converge, offering unprecedented opportunities for companies to innovate and redefine how people interact, transact, and engage. At its core, the metaverse is powered by Web3 technologies like blockchain and NFTs, which enable user ownership, interoperability, and decentralized monetization. Here's a deeper dive into how companies are building their strategies in this space and the resulting business impacts.

Corporate Strategy in the Metaverse

Forward-thinking companies are leveraging the metaverse to create immersive digital environments that cater to a wide range of human activities, such as socializing, gaming, working, shopping, and learning. These environments prioritize decentralization and user ownership, unlocking new ways to engage customers and generate revenue. Examples include:

> **Meta (formerly Facebook):** To dominate the metaverse as the next generation of the internet, where users can interact through virtual reality (VR) and augmented reality (AR). Meta's Horizon Worlds is an interactive platform where users can create, explore, and socialize in

3D spaces. They are also experimenting with blockchain technology to integrate digital asset ownership, potentially enabling NFTs to represent personal avatars, items, or virtual real estate.

- **Epic Games:** To create an open and interoperable metaverse using blockchain to bridge various gaming platforms. Epic Games integrates blockchain technology into its Unreal Engine, enabling developers to create games and experiences where users can own and trade interoperable digital assets, such as skins or in-game items, across different platforms and virtual worlds.

- **Walmart:** To bring the retail shopping experience to the virtual world, allowing users to shop, own, and interact with both physical and digital products. Walmart is developing virtual stores where users can explore products in an immersive environment, buy items as NFTs or physical goods, and participate in gamified shopping experiences.

Key Business Impacts of the Metaverse

New economic models include:

- **Virtual Land and Assets:** Virtual real estate in platforms like Decentraland or The Sandbox is already being bought, sold, and monetized. Companies are purchasing virtual land to build branded experiences, host virtual events, and advertise their products.

- **Digital Collectibles and In-Game Items:** Revenue streams are emerging from in-game purchases, unique NFT-based items, and branded collectibles, many of which continue to generate royalties on secondary sales.

- **Virtual Services and Experiences:** Companies are charging users for access to exclusive virtual concerts, galleries, or training sessions, creating experiential revenue models.

User ownership includes:

- **Empowerment Through NFTs:** NFTs allow users to own digital goods, from virtual land to personal avatars, ensuring that these assets can be sold, traded, or carried across platforms. This ownership fosters deeper engagement as users become stakeholders in the ecosystem.

- **Community-Driven Ecosystems:** With ownership comes a sense of belonging. Companies benefit from engaged communities that actively participate in shaping the metaverse, from contributing user-generated content to advocating for the brand.

Decentralized monetization includes:

- **Earning from UGC (User-Generated Content):** Users can monetize their own creations, such as virtual clothing or 3D assets, with companies taking a share of the transaction fees. This encourages participation and fuels the creation of diverse content.

- **Direct Revenue Streams:** Unlike Web2's centralized ad-based models, Web3-enabled metaverses facilitate direct monetization through sales, subscriptions, or microtransactions without the need for third-party intermediaries.

- **Blockchain-Powered Revenue Sharing:** Decentralized models enable transparent revenue-sharing arrangements between platforms and creators, building trust and sustainable ecosystems.

Additional Use Cases in the Metaverse

- **Virtual Workspaces:** Companies like Microsoft are developing metaverse-based productivity tools where employees can collaborate in immersive virtual environments. Tools like Mesh for Microsoft Teams combine virtual and augmented reality to enable a hybrid work experience.

- **Education and Training:** The metaverse is also reshaping education and training. Businesses can conduct employee training in interactive 3D environments, while educational institutions offer virtual classes and hands-on learning experiences in subjects like medicine or engineering.

- **Advertising and Marketing:** Brands are creating digital billboards, interactive advertisements, and branded virtual experiences within metaverse platforms. These efforts reach a younger, tech-savvy audience in highly engaging ways.

- **Entertainment:** Virtual concerts and festivals are becoming mainstream. For example, Travis Scott's virtual concert in Fortnite attracted millions of viewers and generated significant revenue through ticket and merchandise sales.

Each of these elements—DeFi, NFTs, DAOs, Layer 1 and Layer 2 solutions, and the metaverse—represents a step towards a decentralized internet that prioritizes user control, community governance, and digital ownership. Together, they form the backbone of the Web3 ecosystem, unlocking new possibilities for interacting, transacting, and engaging with digital environments in a decentralized world.

CHAPTER FOUR

Leveraging Data for Profit in Web3

In the Web3 era, data is no longer a resource monopolized by tech giants—it's an asset owned and controlled by individuals. This paradigm shift from Web2's centralized data ownership to Web3's decentralized and monetizable ecosystem has opened immense opportunities for businesses willing to innovate.

> *By adopting blockchain technology, tokens, and decentralized infrastructure, companies have unlocked new ways to engage customers, improve transparency, and monetize data.*

This chapter explores how big players have maximized opportunities in Web3 through applications, decentralized infrastructure networks, and data monetization.

43

Revolutionizing Data with Web3 Applications

Web3 applications showcase the transformative potential of decentralized models, giving users control over their data while enabling companies to innovate in customer engagement and operations. Here's how major brands are leading the charge.

NFTs as Engagement Tools

Big companies are using **non-fungible tokens (NFTs)** to reimagine customer loyalty and engagement. These digital assets serve as a bridge between physical and digital experiences, creating lasting value for both brands and users:

- **Mazda NFTs:** Mazda introduced NFTs that go beyond collectibles, offering exclusive event access and real-world rewards. These "phygital" NFTs merge physical and digital experiences, enhancing brand loyalty and creating new revenue streams.

- **Adidas and Phygital NFTs:** Adidas experimented with NFTs that grant holders exclusive access to limited-edition merchandise and events, validated through blockchain ownership.

Phygital NFTs create immersive, data-driven experiences that reward customer loyalty while giving users tangible ownership of their digital assets.

Web3-powered **travel insurance** revolutionizes the industry with automated claims and payouts. Blockchain-based travel insurance relies on smart contracts. If a flight is delayed or canceled, the smart contract automatically processes the claim and pays out. This approach eliminates intermediaries, lowers costs, and builds trust through transparency.

By automating data-driven processes with smart contracts, companies can streamline operations, reduce costs, and offer seamless user experiences.

Leveraging Decentralized Infrastructure for Competitive Advantage

Decentralized Physical Infrastructure Networks (DePINs) offer companies a decentralized alternative to traditional cloud computing, storage, and Artificial Intelligence (AI) services. By distributing resources across a network of participants, companies gain resilience, scalability, and user trust:

- **Compute and Storage:** Businesses like **Filecoin** allow users to rent out unused computing and storage capacity in exchange for tokens. This decentralized system reduces dependency on centralized providers while lowering costs.

- **AI-Powered Solutions:** DePIN supports decentralized AI applications, processing data locally to preserve privacy while reducing latency. This setup is particularly beneficial for industries requiring real-time analytics, such as healthcare or logistics.

Decentralized infrastructure enables companies to reduce operational costs, increase resilience, and offer user-centric services, all while aligning with Web3's ethos of ownership and transparency.

Turning a Liability into an Asset

In Web2, companies monetized data without user input, leading to concerns over privacy and exploitation. In Web3, companies are flipping the script by allowing users to own and monetize their data, aligning incentives for both businesses and consumers.

- **Tokenized Data Monetization:** Big companies are exploring decentralized platforms to incentivize data sharing. Decentralized Autonomous Organizations (DAOs) offer a collaborative model for monetizing data. Members contribute anonymized datasets in exchange for tokens, creating a shared economy of data ownership. For example, **Ocean Protocol** allows businesses and users to exchange datasets securely while rewarding participants with tokens.

- **Web3 loyalty programs** replace traditional point systems with token-based rewards that are interoperable across platforms. For example, a customer earning loyalty tokens from a coffee chain could use those tokens to purchase a concert ticket, creating a seamless, cross-platform ecosystem.

Tokenized loyalty programs deepen customer engagement, offer flexibility, and allow companies to integrate into broader Web3 ecosystems.

Web3 transforms eCommerce by giving users control over their data. For example, companies can reward customers with tokens for sharing browsing or purchase data, turning data sharing into an economic opportunity. This transparency builds trust while incentivizing participation.

Empowering users to monetize their data fosters trust and positions companies as pioneers in a fair, decentralized economy.

How Big Brands Are Winning in Web3

Many major brands have already reaped the benefits of integrating Web3 applications into their strategies.

Commercial NFT Initiatives:

Brand	NFT Type	Project Name	Launch Date
Adidas	Drop	Into the Metaverse	December 2021
Disney	Drop	Marvel Comics	August 2021
Nike (RTFKT Studio)	Drop	CloneX	November 2021
PepsiCo	Drop	Pepsi Mic Drop	December 2021

These projects have helped companies build stronger brand affinity and generate new revenue streams.

Charity NFT Projects:

Brand	NFT Type	Project Name	Launch Date
Coca-Cola	Auction	Friendship Day Box	July 2021
Kia America	Auction + Drop	Generative Robo Dog	February 2022

By using NFTs for charitable initiatives, brands demonstrate their alignment with socially conscious values, engaging communities in meaningful ways.

Making Data a Competitive Edge

Web3 redefines data's role, turning it into an asset that benefits users and businesses alike. Companies that successfully adapt their strategies to Web3 have achieved:

- **Increased Customer Loyalty:** By giving users ownership of digital assets and tokens, businesses are fostering deeper connections with their audience.

- **New Revenue Streams:** NFTs, decentralized infrastructure, and tokenized data models create new pathways for monetization.

- **Enhanced Transparency:** Blockchain technology enables trust through immutable records, increasing customer confidence.

For companies entering the Web3 space, the ability to leverage decentralized data models and user ownership is not just an opportunity—it's a necessity for staying competitive in the rapidly evolving digital economy.

CHAPTER FIVE

The Convergence of AI

The intersection of Web3 and AI creates unprecedented opportunities for companies to innovate, scale, and dominate emerging markets. In a world defined by decentralization, user ownership, and data sovereignty, AI amplifies the potential of Web3 by enabling personalized, efficient, and autonomous experiences. For large corporations, this convergence offers a roadmap to reshape business models, enhance user engagement, and create new revenue streams.

Here's how big players are harnessing AI in the Web3 space, particularly in the metaverse, decentralized finance (DeFi), and user-centric digital environments.

AI in the Metaverse

Companies are deploying AI to power the next generation of immersive virtual worlds in the metaverse. By leveraging AI's capacity to analyze vast datasets in real time, these firms are creating dynamic, responsive digital spaces that cater to user preferences. Examples include:

- **Meta (formerly Facebook):** Utilizing AI to design virtual environments that adapt to user interactions, enhancing social and professional engagements.

- **Epic Games:** Integrating AI into its Unreal Engine for lifelike characters and immersive, personalized game worlds.

- **NVIDIA:** Driving AI-powered tools like Omniverse to enable creators to build realistic virtual simulations and environments.

The business impact is:

- **Enhanced Engagement:** AI-driven personalization increases user satisfaction and retention by delivering tailored experiences.

- **Efficient Development:** AI tools reduce development timelines, enabling rapid iteration of metaverse features.

- **New Revenue Streams:** Virtual real estate, interactive experiences, and AI-enhanced avatars open lucrative opportunities for monetization.

AI-Driven Personalization

In Web3, personalization is shifting from centralized platforms to user-controlled models. Companies are leveraging AI to deliver hyper-personalized experiences without compromising user privacy, aligning with Web3's ethos of data sovereignty. Examples include:

- **Netflix and Spotify's Web3 Ventures:** Moving beyond traditional recommendation engines, these companies are exploring AI models that offer personalized content tied to user-owned data.

- **Decentraland:** Employing AI to create adaptive virtual spaces where user preferences shape the environment in real time.

The business impact is:

- **User Trust:** AI-driven personalization in Web3 prioritizes privacy, fostering trust and loyalty.

- **Competitive Advantage:** Companies that offer immersive, personalized experiences differentiate themselves in a crowded market.

- **Data Monetization:** AI tools allow users to benefit directly from their data, creating opportunities for companies to partner with users rather than exploit them.

AI-Powered Economies

Companies are integrating AI into decentralized finance (DeFi) and decentralized autonomous organizations (DAOs) to improve efficiency, automation, and decision-making. Examples include:

- **Goldman Sachs and DeFi Investments:** Exploring AI-driven DeFi protocols to automate trading strategies and optimize liquidity pools.

- **DAOs like MakerDAO:** Using AI to analyze market conditions and guide algorithmic governance, ensuring stable and efficient decentralized decision-making.

The business impact is:

- **Optimized Financial Systems:** AI enhances automated market makers (AMMs) and predictive analytics, driving better performance in DeFi protocols.

- **Transparent Governance:** AI-powered insights improve DAO operations, fostering community-driven decisions backed by real-time data.

- **Efficiency Gains:** Companies reduce costs by replacing traditional middlemen with AI-driven smart contracts and algorithms.

Scaling Web3 with AI

AI is playing a critical role in addressing the scalability challenges of Web3, particularly in blockchain networks and decentralized applications (dApps). Companies are using AI to optimize resource allocation, transaction throughput, and energy efficiency. Examples include:

- **IBM:** Partnering with blockchain platforms to use AI for predictive maintenance and resource allocation in decentralized networks.

- **Chainlink:** Incorporating AI to enhance the reliability and accuracy of decentralized oracle services.

The business impact is:

- **Scalability:** AI enables faster, more efficient blockchain networks, supporting mass adoption.

- **Energy Efficiency:** By optimizing computations, AI reduces the environmental impact of blockchain operations.

- **Seamless Interoperability:** AI bridges gaps between blockchain ecosystems, allowing assets and data to move freely.

Transforming Digital Ownership with AI

Companies are redefining digital ownership by integrating AI with NFTs, enabling intelligent, customizable digital assets. Examples include:

- **Adobe:** Introducing AI tools for NFT creators, allowing them to add interactive and programmable elements to digital art.

- **Gaming Giants:** Companies like Ubisoft and Square Enix are using AI to make in-game NFTs adaptive, evolving based on player behavior.

The business impact is:

- **Dynamic Assets:** AI-enhanced NFTs can change and grow over time, increasing their value and utility.

- **User Empowerment:** By combining AI with decentralized ownership, users gain control over smarter, more functional digital assets.

- **Expanded Use Cases:** Intelligent NFTs (iNFTs) unlock new opportunities in gaming, education, and entertainment.

Winning in AI and Web3 Convergence

- **User-Centric Innovation:** By combining AI with Web3's focus on decentralization, companies are enhancing user experiences and driving loyalty.

- **Operational Efficiency:** AI reduces costs, accelerates development, and streamlines governance in decentralized systems.

- **Monetization Opportunities:** The synergy between AI and Web3 enables businesses to create and capture value in new, decentralized economies.

Big companies entering this space are not just adopting Web3 principles—they are actively reshaping their strategies to lead the transition. By leveraging AI as a transformative force within Web3, these firms are paving the way for a decentralized internet that empowers both users and corporations to thrive in an intelligent, democratized digital future.

CHAPTER SIX

Digital Twins and AI Avatars

Т he evolution from Web2 to Web3 has unlocked groundbreaking opportunities for businesses to reimagine user engagement and digital presence. Central to this transformation are **AI-driven avatars** and **digital twins**, which enable immersive, personalized experiences in decentralized environments. For corporations, these technologies aren't just tools for innovation—they're lucrative pathways to dominate the next iteration of the internet.

Here's how big companies are leveraging AI-driven avatars and digital twins to redefine engagement, drive revenue, and build enduring user loyalty.

Personalizing the User Experience

Digital twins are virtual representations of real-world entities, replicating behaviors, preferences, and actions. In Web3, they act as an extension of a user's digital and physical life. Unlike Web2's centralized data-collection systems, Web3 enables users to own their digital twins, giving them control over how their data is used. Examples include:

- **Tesla and BMW:** Using digital twins to create immersive, user-specific virtual car experiences in the metaverse, allowing customers to "test drive" vehicles in a hyper-realistic environment.

- **Healthcare Companies:** Simulating patient profiles through digital twins for personalized treatment in virtual wellness platforms, enabling real-time health monitoring powered by blockchain for data security.

The business impact is:

- **Customer Personalization:** Companies monetize tailored digital experiences, such as offering premium features or exclusive environments in the metaverse.

- **Enhanced Product Testing:** Digital twins allow users to interact with products virtually before purchase, reducing return rates and improving customer satisfaction.

- **Data-Driven Insights:** By analyzing real-time digital twin data, businesses can develop hyper-targeted marketing strategies.

Extending User Autonomy

In Web3, AI-powered avatars go beyond being mere digital representations—they are interactive, evolving extensions of users. These avatars adapt to user preferences, make decisions, and engage autonomously across platforms. For businesses, they offer a unique way to deepen customer engagement and build loyalty. Examples include:

- **Meta (formerly Facebook):** Integrating AI avatars into its metaverse to facilitate virtual meetings, gaming, and socializing, offering premium avatar customization for a fee.

- **Gaming Platforms (Epic Games):** AI-driven avatars in gaming worlds learn from user behavior, offering dynamic experiences and unlocking new in-game purchases based on personalized strategies.

The business impact is:

- **In-Platform Transactions:** Companies generate revenue through microtransactions for avatar upgrades, skins, or exclusive abilities.

- **Subscription Models:** Offering AI-powered avatars as a subscription service with advanced features like dynamic learning or cross-platform interoperability.

- **Brand Collaboration:** Partnering with luxury brands or content creators to create exclusive AI avatar merchandise, driving cross-industry synergies.

Fueling Immersive Digital Twins

Digital twins and avatars thrive on real-world data, creating experiences that feel authentic and tailored. Machine learning algorithms process this data to adapt digital twins to user preferences, enabling highly engaging interactions. Examples include:

- **Nike:** Using customer data to create personalized digital twins for virtual try-ons in the metaverse, allowing users to "wear" and test sneakers before buying.

- **Amazon:** Building AI avatars that guide users through virtual shopping aisles, using past purchase history to suggest personalized product recommendations.

The business impact is:

- **Upselling Opportunities:** By leveraging user data, companies can offer hyper-targeted upsells based on digital twin behavior.

- **Metaverse Advertising:** Digital twins open doors for immersive ad placements tailored to individual preferences, driving higher engagement rates than traditional ads.

- **Data Monetization:** Businesses can offer anonymized, aggregated digital twin data insights to advertisers or developers, all while adhering to Web3's privacy principles.

Ethical AI and User Privacy

For businesses, gaining user trust is paramount in Web3. AI-driven avatars and digital twins require personal data to deliver meaningful experiences, but mishandling this data can lead to reputational damage. Examples include:

- **Apple:** Positioned itself as a privacy-first company, leveraging blockchain solutions for secure data processing while building immersive avatar-driven services.

- **Microsoft:** Integrating decentralized identity tools into its Web3 platforms, ensuring users control access to their digital twins and avatars.

The business impact is:

- **Trust-Driven Growth:** Companies prioritizing ethical AI attract privacy-conscious users willing to pay for secure, premium experiences.

- **Community Governance Models:** Using decentralized governance (e.g., DAOs) to oversee AI transparency creates brand goodwill and builds loyal user communities.

Monetizing AI in Virtual Worlds

AI-driven avatars and digital twins are at the heart of the metaverse economy. Companies use them to create immersive shopping, gaming, and social experiences. Examples include:

- **Walmart:** Developing virtual stores where users can shop with AI avatars that assist with personalized recommendations.

- **Gucci:** Offering NFT-backed digital twins of luxury goods, allowing users to own virtual versions of real-world products.

The business impact is:

- **Virtual Real Estate:** Businesses are selling NFT-based land in the metaverse, powered by interactive digital twins to simulate physical experiences.

- **Event Monetization:** AI avatars enhance virtual event participation, driving ticket sales, sponsorships, and exclusive content access.

Ethical Oversight and Blockchain Security

Blockchain technology offers companies a foundation to handle data ethically while empowering users with ownership. Companies that integrate ethical AI practices position themselves as leaders in Web3's community-driven ecosystem. Examples include:

- **IBM:** Providing blockchain-based identity solutions that enable users to securely control their digital twins in enterprise environments.

- **Sony:** Using blockchain to create tamper-proof, user-controlled digital profiles for enhanced gaming experiences.

The business impact is:

- **Premium Security Features:** Offering advanced encryption or identity management as a paid service.

- **Transparency as a Service:** Allowing enterprises to license blockchain-based tools that ensure ethical data handling.

Big Companies, Big Wins in Web3

AI-driven avatars and digital twins are redefining user engagement in Web3, offering businesses unparalleled opportunities to monetize the next-generation internet. From hyper-personalized shopping experiences to immersive virtual interactions, these technologies enable corporations to unlock new revenue streams while adhering to the principles of decentralization and user control.

The companies that succeed in Web3 are those that not only innovate but also embrace transparency, trust, and ethical practices. By leveraging AI and digital twins, businesses can create meaningful, user-first experiences that secure their position at the forefront of the Web3 revolution. For big brands, the question isn't whether to enter the Web3 space—it's how quickly they can adapt to dominate it.

CHAPTER SEVEN

Decentralized Data, Centralized Profits

The Web3-powered metaverse offers a paradigm shift in how data is handled, creating new opportunities for companies to innovate and generate value while respecting user privacy and ownership. Unlike Web2's centralized approach—dominated by giants like Google and Facebook, where user data is monetized without direct consent—the Web3 metaverse prioritizes user empowerment, data sovereignty, and privacy.

Big corporations entering this space are leveraging these principles to redefine how they engage with users, secure trust, and build lucrative business models.

Here's how major players are successfully navigating and capitalizing on data privacy and security within the Web3 metaverse.

Data Sovereignty

Web2 companies have traditionally profited from user data by centralizing control. In contrast, the Web3 metaverse's decentralized model flips the script, offering businesses new ways to align with consumer demands for ownership and transparency while driving innovation. Examples include:

- **Microsoft:** By integrating blockchain technology in its Azure platform, Microsoft enables enterprises to offer decentralized identity solutions, allowing users to control their personal data while still participating in digital ecosystems.

- **Apple:** Known for its privacy-first branding, Apple is exploring blockchain-based user authentication systems, positioning itself as a leader in secure, decentralized data management.

The business impact is:

- **Revenue Streams from Premium Privacy Features:** Companies can charge users and enterprises for tools that ensure compliance with data sovereignty regulations and provide enhanced control over digital identities.

- **Customer Trust as a Competitive Edge:** Transparent data practices foster loyalty, translating to long-term customer retention and increased market share.

Blockchain and Privacy-First Technologies

Big companies are leveraging privacy-focused blockchain technologies to create secure yet transparent environments for users, allowing them to interact freely in the metaverse while protecting sensitive information. Examples include:

- **Meta (formerly Facebook):** Despite its Web2 roots, Meta is investing in zero-knowledge proof (ZKP) technology to enable private transactions and identity verification within its metaverse projects.

- **IBM:** Through its Hyperledger platform, IBM is integrating homomorphic encryption into enterprise-grade solutions, enabling secure computations on encrypted data for metaverse applications.

The business impact is:

- **Trust-Based Monetization:** By offering privacy-first tools, companies can charge premiums for secure transactions, identity services, and enterprise-level compliance solutions.

- **Strategic Partnerships:** Privacy technologies like ZKPs enable partnerships with governments, healthcare providers, and financial institutions to create tailored, privacy-compliant solutions.

Anonymity and Ownership

Data ownership and anonymity are among Web3's most promising yet challenging aspects. Companies that address these complexities can build trust and new profit avenues in the metaverse. Examples include:

- **Sony Music:** By tokenizing ownership of user-generated music as NFTs, Sony enables artists to retain royalties and monetize directly from their fans, bypassing traditional intermediaries.

- **Nike:** Its NFT-based digital sneakers give users true ownership of virtual assets while allowing Nike to earn ongoing royalties on secondary sales.

- **Chainalysis:** By developing tools that analyze blockchain data for Anti-Money Laundering (AML) compliance while preserving user pseudonymity, Chainalysis supports regulatory compliance without compromising Web3's ethos.

The business impact is:

- **Recurring Revenue Streams:** Tokenized ownership enables companies to earn perpetual royalties and transaction fees.

- **Regulatory Partnerships:** Offering solutions that maintain privacy while ensuring compliance strengthens relationships with governments and institutional clients.

Balancing Transparency and Privacy for Mass Adoption

In the metaverse, transparency and privacy are often seen as opposing forces. Companies that effectively balance these can unlock mass adoption and dominate Web3 markets. Examples include:

- **Amazon:** Exploring blockchain-based supply chain tracking that ensures transparency for consumers while safeguarding proprietary data.

- **Adobe:** Introducing tools that allow content creators to verify and watermark their digital works, ensuring traceability and ownership without exposing personal data.

The business impact is:

- **Enhanced User Engagement:** Transparency in operations, paired with privacy-first tools, drives consumer trust and interaction.

- **Scaling Opportunities:** Privacy features encourage hesitant users and enterprises to adopt Web3 technologies, accelerating market growth.

Privacy-Driven Revenue Models in the Web3 Metaverse

Big companies are using data privacy not just as a regulatory necessity but as a key differentiator to monetize their offerings. Examples include:

- **Premium Data Control Services:** Offering tools for users to manage and monetize their own data. For example, decentralized identity solutions can be monetized as subscriptions or enterprise packages.

- **Privacy-Based Advertising:** Creating systems where users are compensated for sharing anonymized data, turning ads into mutually beneficial transactions.

- **NFT-Driven Revenue:** Allowing creators and users to tokenize their assets ensures companies earn from every transaction while empowering users to participate directly in value creation.

Data Privacy as the Future of Digital Commerce

The Web3 metaverse represents a dramatic shift from Web2's centralized, opaque data models to decentralized, privacy-first ecosystems.

Big companies that adapt to these changes are not only fostering user trust but also creating new revenue streams.

By leveraging data sovereignty, privacy technologies, and tokenized ownership, they are positioning themselves as leaders in a decentralized digital economy.

As the Web3 space evolves, businesses must continue balancing transparency, security, and ethical principles to maintain competitive advantages while addressing user concerns. Those who succeed will set the standard for the next generation of digital engagement, redefining the relationship between users, data, and commerce.

CHAPTER EIGHT

AI-Driven Smart Contracts and Governance

The transition to Web3 has unlocked a new internet paradigm, shifting power from centralized platforms to decentralized ecosystems. Central to this revolution are **smart contracts**—self-executing agreements powered by blockchain.

> *When combined with AI, smart contracts become dynamic and responsive, enabling businesses to automate processes, optimize decision-making, and secure transactions at an unprecedented scale.*

Large corporations entering the Web3 space are leveraging these advancements to enhance operational efficiency, deliver innovative products, and redefine governance models.

This chapter explores how big companies are driving innovation through AI-enhanced smart contracts, oracles, and decentralized governance structures.

AI-Enhanced Smart Contracts

For large enterprises, integrating AI into smart contracts has become a game-changer. Traditional contracts rely on intermediaries for execution, verification, and enforcement. Web3's smart contracts remove these intermediaries, executing agreements automatically based on predefined conditions. AI adds a layer of intelligence, allowing these contracts to analyze data, adapt to real-time changes, and optimize outcomes.

Here is how big companies are applying AI in smart contracts:

- **Dynamic Financial Operations:** DeFi platforms backed by major firms like **Coinbase** or **PayPal** use AI-enhanced smart contracts to dynamically adjust interest rates based on market conditions. This improves efficiency and ensures alignment with real-time economic trends without human intervention.

- **Predictive Insurance Models:** Companies like **Axa** use AI-driven smart contracts for parametric insurance. These contracts automatically release payouts based on external conditions, such as weather data, analyzed in real-time by AI algorithms. Farmers, for instance, receive compensation during droughts without needing to file claims.

- **Fraud Detection in Financial Systems:** AI-enabled anomaly detection in smart contracts helps companies like **Visa** identify suspicious transaction patterns. This capability strengthens security in large-scale DeFi systems.

The business impact is:

- **Operational Efficiency:** Automates routine processes, reducing costs and minimizing delays.

- **Scalability:** Enables businesses to handle large transaction volumes seamlessly.

- **Risk Mitigation:** AI continuously monitors data and flags anomalies, securing systems against fraud and errors.

Bridging On-Chain and Off-Chain Worlds

Smart contracts often rely on real-world data—such as stock prices, weather updates, or logistics information—to execute. Oracles serve as the bridge between blockchain and external data sources. When paired with AI, oracles become more reliable, secure, and capable of interpreting complex data.

The corporate applications of AI-powered oracles are:

- **Supply Chain Management:** Companies like **IBM** use AI-enhanced oracles in their blockchain-based supply chain solutions to track shipments. AI validates and cross-references data, ensuring the accuracy of delivery timelines and inventory updates.

- **Financial Data Integration: Goldman Sachs** leverages AI-powered oracles to feed accurate stock market data into blockchain-based financial instruments. This allows for real-time settlement of trades and automated portfolio adjustments.

- **Dynamic Content Licensing:** Streaming platforms like **Spotify** use AI oracles to verify licensing agreements dynamically. AI interprets streaming data to trigger royalty payments to artists based on real-time usage.

The business impact is:

- **Data Accuracy:** Cross-referencing multiple data sources ensures reliability.

- **Expanded Use Cases:** Enables contracts to process complex inputs like sentiment analysis or weather forecasts.

- **Enhanced Security:** AI detects and prevents data manipulation, safeguarding sensitive business operations.

AI in DAO Governance

Decentralized Autonomous Organizations (DAOs) are at the forefront of Web3 governance, offering transparency and inclusivity. However, scaling governance to meet corporate needs often introduces challenges, such as inefficiencies in decision-making or susceptibility to manipulation. AI is helping companies streamline DAO governance, making it more effective and scalable.

The corporate use of AI in DAO governance includes:

- **Automating Proposal Evaluation: Uniswap Labs**, a leader in decentralized exchanges, uses AI to rank governance proposals. Proposals with low impact or redundancies are deprioritized, ensuring efficient use of community voting time.

- **Real-Time Sentiment Analysis: Meta (formerly Facebook)** integrates AI tools to analyze sentiment around governance discussions within its emerging DAO experiments. This helps prioritize features that align with user preferences.

- **Fair Voting Mechanisms:** Gaming DAOs backed by **Epic Games** use AI to analyze voting patterns and prevent collusion, ensuring equitable decision-making in platform governance.

- **Predictive Analytics for Strategic Planning:** Investment DAOs like **The LAO**, which funds Web3 startups, use AI to assess potential ROI based on historical funding data, guiding communities toward informed decisions.

The business impact is:

- **Increased Efficiency:** Speeds up decision-making processes by automating routine evaluations.

- **Community Alignment:** Ensures governance decisions reflect member sentiment and long-term goals.

- **Security:** Detects and prevents vote manipulation or governance breaches.

Corporate Gains from AI in Web3

By embedding AI into Web3 infrastructure, companies are unlocking a suite of competitive advantages:

- **Enhanced Automation:** AI-driven smart contracts and governance reduce reliance on human intervention, saving costs and improving accuracy.

- **Deeper User Engagement:** AI-powered oracles and governance models allow businesses to respond to user preferences and feedback in real time.

- **Scalability and Security:** AI systems scale effortlessly while protecting systems from fraud and manipulation.

Building the Future of Decentralized Business

AI-powered smart contracts and governance tools have become indispensable for corporations entering Web3. By leveraging AI in critical areas such as contract automation, data integration, and governance, companies are reshaping their business models to align with the decentralized ethos of Web3. This fusion of AI and blockchain enables businesses to:

- Innovate faster.
- Build stronger, trust-based ecosystems.
- Scale operations to meet global demands.

As companies like **Visa, Meta, Goldman Sachs**, and **IBM** demonstrate, the integration of AI into Web3 is not just a technological upgrade—it's a strategic advantage that will define market leaders in the digital economy of the future.

CHAPTER NINE

Portable Identities, Profitable Futures

The shift to Web3 presents a transformative opportunity for businesses to capitalize on decentralized data ownership and portability. In Web3, control over data moves from centralized platforms to users, enabling a freer, more user-focused internet. Big companies that recognize and embrace these principles are redefining their business models to enhance user trust, expand digital ecosystems, and monetize data in revolutionary ways. Let's examine how major players are leveraging Web3's data portability and sovereignty to unlock growth and value.

Data Portability in Web3

For decades, Web2 companies like Facebook and Google have controlled user data within their ecosystems, creating "walled gardens" that restrict data sharing. In Web3, data portability shatters these barriers, empowering users to carry their digital identities and assets seamlessly across platforms. Forward-thinking companies are using this shift to create interoperable ecosystems, increase user retention, and tap into new revenue streams. Examples include:

- **Gaming and Entertainment:** Companies like **Epic Games** are integrating decentralized identities into their platforms, allowing gamers to port avatars, achievements, and in-game assets between titles and even across metaverse platforms like **Decentraland**. This strategy keeps users engaged while fostering loyalty in an increasingly decentralized ecosystem.

- **Enterprise Collaboration Tools: Microsoft** is exploring decentralized identity systems to enable seamless integration between enterprise tools. With users owning their profiles, credentials, and documents, businesses can reduce onboarding friction and foster long-term productivity.

Decentralized Identifiers (DIDs)

DIDs are a revolutionary tool enabling companies to streamline user interactions while respecting data sovereignty. Instead of siloed identities managed by platforms, DIDs offer users a portable, blockchain-based identity layer that spans applications and ecosystems. For example, Adobe is integrating DIDs into its creative suite tools, allowing artists to authenticate and carry their digital portfolios across platforms. For example, a creator could use their DID to verify their work on **OpenSea** or other NFT marketplaces, fostering cross-platform recognition and monetization opportunities.

By adopting DIDs, companies reduce costs associated with maintaining identity systems while empowering users to build trust and loyalty through control of their digital presence. This approach aligns with Web3's ethos while enhancing the user experience.

Personal Data Stores

Personal data stores represent a significant opportunity for companies to innovate their data strategies. These decentralized vaults enable users to securely store and manage their data, granting or revoking access to specific parties. For example, **Spotify** could leverage personal data stores to allow users to share listening preferences directly with artists or brands for tailored recommendations while ensuring that data remains under the user's control. This model creates trust and transparency, attracting privacy-conscious users.

In terms of healthcare, companies like **IBM** are piloting personal data stores in healthcare, enabling patients to securely share medical records with providers, researchers, or insurers as needed. This approach not only enhances privacy but also creates new revenue opportunities for facilitating trusted data sharing.

Tokenized Data Ownership

Web3's tokenization capabilities enable companies to offer users ownership over their data and a share in its value. By tokenizing data, businesses can create transparent marketplaces where users directly benefit from their contributions. For example, social media platforms like **Reddit** are experimenting with tokenized user engagement. Content creators can tokenize their posts, allowing them to sell or license popular content, with platforms taking a smaller fee compared to traditional ad-based revenue models.

Enterprises like **Salesforce** can implement tokenized data systems that allow businesses to trade anonymized, aggregated data sets on decentralized marketplaces. This approach ensures transparency while creating new income streams for users and businesses alike.

Monetizing Data Sovereignty

In Web3, companies can align user incentives with their own by building transparent systems for data monetization. Instead of exploiting user data for advertising revenue, Web3 models enable users to license their data directly, fostering a sense of collaboration. For example, **Procter & Gamble (P&G)** could use tokenized data markets to reward users for sharing purchase preferences or feedback. This data could then inform product development, creating a direct and transparent value exchange between the company and consumers.

Platforms like **Ocean Protocol** are being adopted by enterprises to enable secure and direct transactions of user data. These marketplaces eliminate intermediaries, ensuring fair compensation for both parties.

The Competitive Advantage of Data Sovereignty

Big companies adopting Web3 principles are seeing more than just financial returns—they're fostering user trust, loyalty, and engagement by empowering individuals with control over their digital lives.

> *Data sovereignty enables enterprises to position themselves as champions of transparency and user-centric innovation.*

For example, **Visa** is experimenting with tokenized financial data, allowing users to maintain ownership of their transaction histories while selectively sharing information for credit assessments or rewards programs. This approach aligns with user demands for privacy while creating value-added services.

Companies embracing data sovereignty, such as **Apple** with its privacy-focused initiatives, are building long-term trust with users, creating competitive advantages in increasingly data-conscious markets.

Looking Ahead: A Decentralized Future

As Web3 continues to mature, data portability and sovereignty are becoming non-negotiable for companies seeking to thrive in the decentralized economy. From enabling seamless cross-platform experiences to monetizing user data transparently, these concepts are reshaping how businesses engage with consumers.

Key Takeaways for Enterprises

- **Embrace Interoperability:** Investing in decentralized identifiers and data portability solutions fosters loyalty and user retention.

- **Empower Users:** Providing tools like personal data stores or tokenized data ownership builds trust and enhances user engagement.

- **Monetize Transparently:** Create win-win scenarios by aligning user incentives with new monetization models.

Big companies entering Web3 are not just adapting—they're leading. By integrating data portability and sovereignty into their strategies, they're unlocking new revenue streams, building deeper user relationships, and positioning themselves at the forefront of the next internet revolution.

CHAPTER TEN

Real-Time Data Analytics in the Metaverse

The Web3-powered metaverse offers businesses a goldmine of real-time data analytics. Unlike the Web2 ecosystem—where platforms monopolize user data—Web3 decentralizes control, allowing businesses to directly access data generated through blockchain-based interactions. Companies are leveraging this democratized data flow to drive customer engagement, optimize operations, and unlock new monetization opportunities. For example:

- **Meta (formerly Facebook):** By building immersive metaverse environments, Meta collects interaction and transaction data in real time, helping advertisers target users in a decentralized yet highly engaging manner.

- **Nike and RTFKT:** These brands track user preferences for virtual sneakers and accessories, using the data to refine future NFT drops and metaverse campaigns.

- **Gaming Companies (e.g., Roblox, Epic Games):** By integrating blockchain data, they analyze player behaviors and asset usage, creating tailored gaming experiences and incentivized token economies.

Big companies are creating detailed digital engagement maps, helping them understand where and how users spend their time and resources in the metaverse.

AI-Driven Real-Time Insights

The big players use AI to customize the user experience. Businesses use AI to analyze real-time data streams, adjusting virtual environments to user preferences dynamically. For example:

- **Gucci:** In metaverse platforms like Roblox, Gucci customizes virtual store layouts based on visitor behavior and engagement patterns.

- **Amazon:** Exploring metaverse retail opportunities, Amazon could use real-time data to personalize product displays, just as it does with its Web2 marketplace.

Web3 shifts the paradigm by letting users actively participate in data monetization. Brands partner with users by offering token-based rewards for sharing insights, turning data ownership into a collaborative effort. For example, Starbucks integrates Web3 concepts, rewarding users with NFTs and tokens for engagement, creating a two-way value exchange. Also, companies like Microsoft analyze in-the-moment data to optimize virtual meetings and event scheduling in metaverse spaces, improving productivity and engagement.

The business impact is:

- Increased customer retention through hyper-personalized interactions.

- Efficient allocation of resources for promotions, events, and updates.

- Greater user trust and collaboration due to transparent, incentive-driven data sharing.

Predictive Analytics

Big companies are harnessing predictive analytics to stay ahead in the fast-evolving Web3 landscape. AI-powered algorithms analyze historical and real-time data to forecast trends in user behavior, virtual asset values, and engagement patterns. The virtual market trends include:

- **Real Estate:** Predictive tools help companies like Decentraland and The Sandbox identify high-demand virtual land areas, informing investment decisions.

- **Digital Commerce:** Retailers predict which virtual goods (e.g., skins, NFTs) are likely to trend, optimizing production and marketing strategies.

Financial giants like JPMorgan and PayPal use blockchain-based predictive analytics to anticipate market fluctuations in metaverse tokens and assets. This empowers both companies and their customers to make informed trading and investment decisions.

DAOs, supported by predictive analytics, improve decision-making processes by forecasting the outcomes of governance votes. For example, a DAO managing a metaverse platform could predict how proposed fee changes might impact user retention and adjust accordingly.

The business impact is:

- Enhanced ability to anticipate user needs and market shifts.

- Improved ROI on virtual investments, from digital items to real estate.

- Greater transparency and user trust in governance and economic systems.

Real-Time Data as a Corporate Resource

Through the metaverse, real-time data analytics is being transformed into a participatory economic asset. Users generate data through every interaction, from shopping in virtual malls to attending concerts or gaming events. Big companies can access this data for a range of purposes:

- **Product Development:** Insights from virtual interactions inform physical-world product design and marketing campaigns.

- **Marketing Strategy:** Brands launch promotions based on peak engagement times and popular activities, ensuring maximum reach.

- **Economic Insights:** By analyzing token movements and asset trading, companies gauge the health of the broader metaverse economy.

Examples include:

- **Coca-Cola:** Leveraging real-time data from NFT campaigns to adjust virtual marketing strategies.

- **Adidas:** Using blockchain analytics to predict future demand for its metaverse wearable collections.

The Future of Big Business in the Metaverse

By combining real-time and predictive analytics, companies operating in the Web3 space are reshaping how digital data is collected, shared, and monetized. This evolution not only allows businesses to tailor experiences in the moment but also empowers them to anticipate trends, ensuring they remain competitive in a rapidly growing digital economy.

Key Takeaways for Enterprises

- **Leverage Real-Time Data:** Enhance customer engagement by dynamically adapting to user needs and preferences in the metaverse.

- **Utilize Predictive Analytics:** Gain foresight into market trends to optimize investments and operational strategies.

- **Foster User Collaboration:** Incentivize data sharing through transparent, token-based rewards, building trust and loyalty.

By embracing these strategies, companies like Meta, Nike, and Microsoft are leading the charge, proving that Web3 and the metaverse are not just buzzwords—they are the next frontier of business innovation.

CHAPTER ELEVEN

Ethical AI and Responsible Data Management

As the Web3 ecosystem continues to evolve, ethical AI and responsible data management are becoming key pillars of success for companies entering this space. In a decentralized, user-owned internet, fairness, inclusivity, and transparency are not just ethical imperatives—they are business necessities. Forward-thinking corporations are using these principles to differentiate themselves, create trust, and build scalable, user-centric systems.

This chapter explores how big companies are navigating the challenges and opportunities of ethical AI in Web3, with practical applications that maximize both innovation and responsibility.

Corporate Integration of Ethical AI in Decentralized Systems

In the Web3 landscape, where decentralization eliminates traditional gatekeepers, companies must rethink how they design and deploy AI. AI systems in Web3 operate autonomously across decentralized platforms, handling critical tasks like identity verification, asset management, and financial transactions. For big businesses, building ethical AI solutions within this framework involves balancing innovation with user trust. Companies apply this through:

- **AI Transparency:** Businesses like **IBM** and **Microsoft** are developing blockchain-based AI tools that log every decision and process, creating auditable trails. This transparency ensures that users can trust the AI systems managing their data and transactions.

- **User Empowerment:** Platforms such as **Coinbase** are leveraging AI to enhance decentralized decision-making, using explainable AI models to help users understand how recommendations or decisions are made in crypto investments or decentralized applications (dApps).

- **Accountability Structures:** Companies are partnering with **Decentralized Autonomous Organizations (DAOs)** to establish decentralized auditing frameworks, ensuring their AI solutions align with community-driven ethical standards.

The business impact is:

- **Enhanced Trust and Adoption:** Transparent AI systems foster trust among users, increasing platform adoption and loyalty.

- **Regulatory Preparedness:** Ethical AI practices help companies comply with emerging Web3-focused regulations, avoiding reputational and financial risks.

- **Competitive Edge:** By positioning themselves as leaders in ethical AI, companies gain an edge in attracting conscientious users and developers.

Tackling AI Bias in Web3

AI bias is a long-standing challenge, and in the decentralized world of Web3, the problem becomes even more complex. Web3 decentralizes data ownership, allowing users to control their data. However, this fragmented model creates the risk of inconsistent or incomplete datasets, which can introduce or exacerbate biases in AI systems. Companies solve this through:

- **Diverse Data Collection:** Companies like **Google Cloud AI** are working with DAOs and open-source communities to source diverse datasets that reflect global user demographics.

- **Bias Audits and Testing:** Platforms such as **OpenAI** are collaborating with blockchain-based projects to perform pre-deployment audits on AI models. These audits identify and mitigate potential biases before deployment, leveraging the immutable nature of blockchain to maintain accountability.

- **Community-Driven Data Governance:** Companies are investing in DAO-led data governance models, where diverse stakeholders contribute to building and curating datasets used for training AI systems. For instance, **Chainlink** enables decentralized data oracles to provide verified and diverse datasets for AI models.

The business impact is:

- **Fairer Systems:** Inclusive AI models reduce the risk of alienating specific user groups, broadening market reach.

- **Stronger Ecosystem Ties:** By involving communities in data governance, companies build deeper relationships with users and developers.

- **Long-Term Viability:** Bias-free systems ensure sustainable growth in diverse global markets.

DAO-Led Ethical AI Standards

Decentralized Autonomous Organizations (DAOs) are reshaping how companies approach governance, including the governance of AI ethics. By giving communities voting power over AI-related policies, companies can create systems that reflect user values while maintaining operational efficiency. Companies use DAOs for Ethical AI through:

- **Ethical Guidelines Creation:** Companies like **Uniswap** are using DAOs to create guidelines for how AI models should handle sensitive user data and decision-making processes.

- **Real-Time Monitoring:** Blockchain-based monitoring tools integrated into DAO frameworks allow companies to ensure compliance with ethical standards. For example, **Aave** uses DAO-driven oversight to manage its decentralized financial protocols, ensuring they operate transparently.

- **Incentivized Oversight:** Through token-based rewards, DAOs incentivize community members to monitor and report any deviations from agreed ethical AI standards.

The business impact is:

- **Shared Responsibility:** DAO involvement reduces the burden on companies to unilaterally govern ethical AI, distributing accountability across the community.

- **Adaptability:** As AI evolves, DAO-led governance can quickly adapt ethical guidelines to address emerging challenges.

- **Enhanced Credibility:** Companies seen as supporting community-driven governance strengthen their reputations in the Web3 space.

The Business of Responsible Data Management

Data management is at the heart of Web3, and big companies are leveraging responsible practices to align with the ecosystem's emphasis on user ownership and control. Ethical AI systems rely on secure, decentralized data storage and processing. Companies manage data responsibly through:

- **Decentralized Data Protocols:** Companies like **Amazon Web Services (AWS)** are providing decentralized storage solutions that ensure data is encrypted and accessible only to authorized users.

- **Consent-Based AI Models:** Startups backed by large corporations, such as **Brave**, are building consent-based AI systems where users explicitly allow their data to be used for training algorithms.

- **Data Privacy Innovations:** Privacy-preserving technologies, such as **zero-knowledge proofs**, are being integrated by companies like **Zcash** to secure user data while enabling AI to perform computations without accessing the raw data.

The business impact is:

- **User Trust:** Privacy-focused systems increase user trust and retention.

- **Operational Security:** Decentralized data storage reduces the risk of data breaches.

- **Regulatory Compliance:** Responsible data management aligns with global privacy laws like GDPR and emerging Web3-specific regulations.

Web3's Ethical AI Opportunity

Big companies entering Web3 have recognized that ethical AI and responsible data management are not just moral imperatives— they are critical to success. By prioritizing transparency, inclusivity, and decentralized governance, these companies are setting the standard for how AI operates in the next generation of the internet.

Through collaborations with DAOs, investments in bias-free AI systems, and commitment to user-centric governance, businesses are leveraging Web3's unique features to enhance their market position. For forward-thinking companies, ethical AI in Web3 is more than a challenge—it's an unparalleled opportunity to lead in a decentralized, user-first digital future.

CHAPTER TWELVE

Tokenized Data and the Virtual Economy

The emergence of Web3, often referred to as the "Ownership Economy," is rewriting the rules of data ownership and monetization. For big companies, this shift represents not just a challenge to the Web2 status quo but a golden opportunity to redefine how value is created and shared.

> *By leveraging tokenization and decentralized technology, forward-thinking corporations are turning data into digital assets, creating new revenue streams, and aligning themselves with the principles of Web3.*

Here's how major players are capitalizing on the tokenized economy and reshaping the virtual economy to their advantage.

Tokenizing Data

Big companies are using blockchain to tokenize data, transforming it into a tradeable, monetizable asset. Instead of exploiting user data, they're enabling value exchange through decentralized platforms, fostering trust and engagement. For example:

- **Brave Browser:** This Web3 browser rewards users with Basic Attention Tokens (BAT) for choosing to share their browsing data with advertisers. This model flips traditional ad revenue models by compensating users directly.

- **Ocean Protocol:** This decentralized data marketplace enables organizations to tokenize and sell datasets while maintaining control over sensitive information, creating new revenue channels.

The business impact is:

- **New Revenue Models:** Companies can tokenize internal datasets or incentivize users to share data, earning transaction fees or royalties on data usage.

- **Enhanced User Trust:** By giving users control over their data, businesses strengthen customer loyalty and brand reputation.

- **Market Expansion:** Tokenized data unlocks access to global markets by creating a standardized, tradeable asset class.

Revolutionizing Ownership and Representation

Companies are leveraging non-fungible tokens (NFTs) to represent ownership of digital assets, from creative works to personal data, opening up innovative monetization opportunities. For example:

- **Nike's Cryptokicks:** By launching NFTs tied to digital sneakers, Nike gives customers both physical and virtual ownership, creating a seamless cross-platform brand experience.

- **Epic Games:** Using NFTs to represent in-game assets, allowing players to trade and monetize items across its gaming ecosystem.

- **Pfizer and Genomics Companies:** Exploring the use of NFTs to tokenize health data, enabling users to own and control access to their personal medical records.

The business impact is:

- **Cross-Platform Monetization:** NFT-based ownership allows assets to be used across multiple platforms, creating interconnected revenue opportunities.

- **Long-Term Loyalty:** By integrating NFTs into customer rewards or membership programs, companies foster deeper brand engagement.

- **Decentralized Creativity:** Corporations are returning ownership to creators—whether artists or consumers—aligning their values with the Web3 ethos of empowerment.

Incentives for Data Sharing

Web3 companies are incentivizing users to share data securely by offering token rewards, creating a transparent and mutually beneficial exchange model. For example:

- **Google's Decentralized Data Projects:** Exploring tokenized incentives for users sharing anonymized data in exchange for rewards or platform benefits.

- **Healthcare Companies:** Offering token-based rewards for participants who provide health data for clinical research, enabling secure and ethical data sharing.

- **Spotify:** Experimenting with blockchain to reward listeners who share data about their preferences and activity patterns.

The business impact is:

- **Direct Data Monetization:** Users receive tokens for sharing data, and companies gain valuable insights for targeted marketing or R&D.

- **Reduced Privacy Risks:** Tokenized, decentralized data-sharing models reduce the likelihood of breaches or misuse, mitigating compliance risks.

- **Community Engagement:** Incentives encourage active participation and data sharing, transforming passive users into active contributors.

Turning Data into Digital Assets

Companies are tokenizing digital and real-world assets, creating verifiable ownership and enabling data to function as collateral or a tradeable asset. For example:

- **Microsoft Azure's Blockchain-as-a-Service (BaaS):** Helping enterprises tokenize assets like intellectual property and supply chain data, enabling secure sharing and trading.

- **Binance NFT Marketplace:** Facilitating the trade of tokenized data and intellectual property, empowering creators and organizations to monetize digital goods.

- **Timbaland's Ape-In Productions:** Using NFTs from the Bored Ape Yacht Club to create content like music and animation, setting a precedent for creator-driven ownership in entertainment.

The business impact is:

- **Expanded Ecosystem Revenue:** Tokenized data assets can be monetized within broader ecosystems, creating interconnected opportunities.

- **Enhanced Collateral Models:** Data-backed tokens enable companies and users to access DeFi services, such as loans or staking.

- **Brand Differentiation:** Companies embracing NFTs signal innovation and align with tech-savvy audiences, strengthening their market position.

Building New Marketplaces

Businesses are creating virtual marketplaces where tokenized assets like data, NFTs, and digital services can be exchanged, driving the growth of the virtual economy. For example:

- **Meta (formerly Facebook):** Pivoting towards the metaverse, where NFTs and tokenized assets serve as the foundation for digital goods and experiences.

- **Decentraland and The Sandbox:** Partnering with brands like Adidas to create virtual spaces where users can trade tokenized assets and interact with brands in immersive environments.

- **Amazon Web Services:** Exploring Web3-enabled marketplaces to tokenize and trade cloud computing resources.

The business impact is:

- **Virtual Commerce Growth:** Companies earn revenue from transaction fees and marketplace activity within virtual environments.

- **Customer Experience Innovation:** By integrating tokenized assets, brands deliver personalized, gamified, and engaging experiences.

- **Global Reach:** Virtual marketplaces operate 24/7, enabling companies to engage with customers across time zones and geographies.

Capitalizing on Web3's Tokenized Economy

Big companies are leveraging Web3's tokenized economy to redefine their role in the digital landscape. By turning data and assets into tradeable tokens, they unlock new revenue streams, foster user trust, and create innovative ecosystems for value exchange. Whether through data tokenization, NFTs, or incentivized data sharing, these corporations are not only aligning with the decentralized values of Web3 but also positioning themselves as leaders in a transformative digital era.

For businesses that embrace Web3, the opportunities are limitless—reshaping digital ownership, monetization, and participation to drive growth and innovation in the virtual economy.

CHAPTER THIRTEEN

The Interoperability Edge

As Web3 redefines the digital landscape with decentralization and user ownership at its core, major corporations are capitalizing on this shift by integrating AI and data interoperability to create seamless, scalable, and user-friendly experiences. By embracing these technologies, big companies are breaking barriers, ensuring cohesion across blockchain ecosystems, and unlocking new revenue streams in the "ownership economy."

Here's how companies are leveraging AI-driven data interoperability to dominate the decentralized space.

AI-Driven Cross-Chain Data Ecosystems

The diverse architectures of blockchains like Ethereum, Solana, and Polkadot have created opportunities for companies to specialize in bridging these siloed ecosystems. AI-powered solutions are enabling seamless asset transfers, cross-platform application interactions, and global scalability. For example:

- **Google Cloud's Blockchain Node Engine:** Providing an interoperable platform for developers across different blockchains, powered by AI to optimize cross-chain compatibility.

- **PayPal's Blockchain Investments:** Facilitating cross-chain payment systems using AI to reduce conversion time and transaction costs.

The business impact is:

- **Streamlined Operations:** By automating data translation between blockchains, companies reduce inefficiencies and open the door to cross-chain business models.

- **Global Reach:** Interoperability solutions allow users to interact across multiple chains, expanding market opportunities for companies offering multi-blockchain services.

Cross-Chain NFT and dApp Interactions

Big brands are leveraging AI to enable cross-chain compatibility for NFTs and decentralized applications (dApps), creating interconnected digital ecosystems. For example:

- **Epic Games:** AI-driven protocols allow NFT items created in their games to function seamlessly across other virtual environments, such as Decentraland or The Sandbox.

- **Nike:** Uses AI-enhanced interoperability solutions to enable users to wear NFT sneakers across multiple metaverse platforms.

The business impact is:

- **Enhanced Asset Utility:** Users gain greater value from their NFTs and other digital assets, increasing brand loyalty.

- **Revenue Expansion:** Cross-platform functionality encourages users to engage with assets in new contexts, driving secondary market sales and royalties.

AI-Driven Consistent User Experiences Across Web3 Platforms

Delivering a unified user experience across decentralized platforms is crucial for mass adoption. Companies are deploying AI to personalize and standardize interactions across blockchains, ensuring continuity and ease of use. For example:

- **Meta's Metaverse Initiatives:** Using AI to synchronize user profiles and digital assets across its Horizon Worlds and third-party platforms.

- **Microsoft's Decentralized Identity (DID) Solutions:** Ensuring seamless cross-platform credential management using AI.

The business impact is:

- **User Retention:** Consistent experiences reduce friction, keeping users engaged across multiple applications.

- **Scalable Personalization:** AI-driven insights allow for dynamic content curation and customized user interfaces across platforms.

The Role of Decentralized Oracles Enhanced by AI

Oracles—systems that connect blockchains to external data—become pivotal when integrated with AI. Companies are using AI-enhanced oracles to provide accurate, standardized data streams to dApps, enabling smooth functionality across platforms. For example:

- **Chainlink:** Incorporating AI to enhance the reliability and standardization of off-chain data fed to various blockchain applications.

- **IBM Blockchain Services:** Developing AI-driven oracle solutions for enterprise-level cross-platform supply chain management.

The business impact is:

- **Operational Efficiency:** Accurate and timely data integration reduces errors, increasing trust in decentralized systems.

- **Cross-Sector Integration:** Oracles powered by AI open opportunities in industries like healthcare, supply chain, and finance, expanding blockchain's use cases.

AI-Enhanced Interoperability as a Growth Catalyst

By solving interoperability challenges, companies can tap into the broader Web3 ecosystem, making decentralized platforms as accessible as Web2 systems while preserving user ownership. For example:

- **Stripe's Crypto Services:** Offering payment gateways compatible across multiple blockchains, enabled by AI for faster conversions.

- **Adobe:** Empowering creators with AI tools for interoperable NFT minting and cross-platform distribution.

The business impact is:

- **Market Expansion:** AI-driven interoperability enables companies to serve diverse user bases across different blockchains, fostering ecosystem-wide growth.

- **Revenue Potential:** With a projected $500 billion in interoperable asset value by 2025 (DappRadar), companies investing in interoperability solutions position themselves at the forefront of a lucrative market.

The Future of AI in Web3 Interoperability

Big corporations recognize the transformative potential of AI in the decentralized space. By ensuring interoperability, they are not only solving one of Web3's greatest technical challenges but also creating a unified, user-friendly digital ecosystem.

The business impact is:

- **Innovation Leadership:** Companies like Microsoft, Google, and Meta are driving the narrative of seamless Web3 experiences, cementing their place as key enablers of the next internet era.

- **Decentralized Accessibility:** AI-powered solutions make Web3 platforms more accessible, bringing the benefits of decentralization to mass audiences.

- **Future-Proofing:** By investing in cross-chain compatibility, businesses future-proof their platforms against fragmentation, ensuring relevance as Web3 evolves.

The Competitive Edge in AI-Powered Web3

By embracing AI and data interoperability, big companies are reshaping the Web3 landscape, unlocking untapped markets, and delivering unparalleled user experiences. As interoperability solutions mature, companies that invest in these technologies today will be the ones dominating the decentralized economy tomorrow.

In this era of the "ownership economy," the seamless integration of blockchain ecosystems powered by AI is not just a technical achievement—it's a strategic imperative for enterprises seeking to thrive in the Web3 revolution.

CHAPTER FOURTEEN

Data Monetization in Web3

Web3 has transformed the concept of data ownership, turning what was once a passive asset exploited by centralized corporations into an active revenue generator for individuals and businesses alike. For large companies, entering the Web3 space has unlocked new monetization models, enhanced consumer engagement, and redefined their approach to data economics.

By adopting Web3's decentralized frameworks, companies have created scalable systems that align with its ethos of user control, transparency, and shared value.

This chapter delves into how big players are leveraging Web3's data monetization opportunities—including decentralized marketplaces, AI-driven insights, and NFT-enabled creator tools—to capture value and innovate in a competitive digital economy.

Reinventing Revenue Models

In Web2, companies monetized user data through targeted advertising and analytics, often without direct benefit to users. Web3 flips the script by introducing tokenized data ownership models that enable shared value creation between companies and users:

- **Big Tech and Data Tokens:** Companies like Google and Meta are exploring Web3-inspired frameworks, enabling users to tokenize their data. For example, a user on a decentralized social platform might earn tokens whenever their data is accessed for advertising or research, creating an entirely new revenue stream.

- **Enterprise Example: Ocean Protocol**, a blockchain-based data marketplace, partners with organizations to tokenize proprietary datasets, allowing companies to profit while giving data owners control over their information. Large corporations are investing in or integrating with platforms like Ocean to stay ahead of the curve.

The business impact is:

- **User-Driven Monetization:** By enabling users to tokenize and sell their data, companies can attract privacy-conscious customers who are empowered to participate in their revenue generation.

- **New Revenue Streams:** Tokenized data assets open up avenues for licensing and fractional ownership, driving innovation in sectors like healthcare, finance, and retail.

- **Brand Loyalty:** Sharing revenue with users enhances trust and fosters deeper customer relationships.

AI-Driven Data Marketplaces

Companies are tapping into AI-powered decentralized marketplaces to securely and transparently trade data, reducing reliance on intermediaries and ensuring ethical usage:

- **AI Insights and Data Sharing:** Platforms like **Fetch.ai** and **SingularityNET** have attracted corporate partners by enabling the buying, selling, and analysis of data with unprecedented efficiency. These marketplaces analyze data demand trends, helping companies target specific datasets for high-value exchanges.

- **Healthcare Example:** A global pharma company might use an AI-driven marketplace to access anonymized health data for research, compensating users directly via smart contracts while ensuring compliance with data privacy laws.

Dynamic monetization models include:

- **Data Rentals:** Users or companies retain ownership while providing temporary access to their data for specified purposes, creating recurring income streams.

- **Smart Contract Automation:** Payments and access terms are governed by blockchain-based contracts, reducing administrative overhead and enhancing transaction security.

The business impact is:

- **Cost Efficiency:** Decentralized marketplaces eliminate intermediaries, reducing the cost of data acquisition.

- **Ethical and Transparent Practices:** Public blockchain ledgers ensure compliance and build trust with stakeholders.

- **Targeted Data Ecosystems:** AI tools optimize the discovery and monetization of high-value data.

Empowering Creators

Big brands are integrating NFTs to enable creators to monetize their work directly while engaging consumers with unique, tradable assets. Companies like **Warner Music Group** and **Disney** are experimenting with NFT-backed fan engagement tools. These allow artists and content creators to sell unique digital assets (e.g., music tracks, collectibles) while earning royalties on secondary market sales. For example, Nike has launched NFT-based digital sneakers that blend physical and virtual ownership. Each Cryptokick allows users to customize and trade their footwear across platforms in the metaverse, fostering new avenues for brand loyalty and revenue.

Dynamic monetization features for creators include:

- **Provenance and Exclusivity:** NFTs establish clear ownership records, which creators and companies can leverage to add value and scarcity.

- **Secondary Market Royalties:** Automated royalty distribution via smart contracts ensures creators profit from every resale of their work, generating long-term revenue.

The business impact is:

- **Market Expansion:** NFTs allow brands to tap into new digital-native audiences while monetizing intellectual property.

- **Stronger Brand Engagement:** Exclusive content and collectibles deepen customer connections, fostering long-term loyalty.

- **Decentralized Revenue Models:** NFTs provide creators and brands with full control over their pricing and revenue strategies, bypassing traditional intermediaries.

Turning Data and Creativity into Revenue

Music industry veteran Timbaland has built a decentralized content ecosystem around Bored Ape Yacht Club NFTs. The platform allows musicians to create and monetize content directly, bypassing record labels and streaming services. By leveraging NFTs for ownership and revenue sharing, Timbaland empowers artists to profit fully from their creativity while connecting with fans in innovative ways.

The business impact is:

- **Ownership Economy at Scale:** Big brands can replicate this model by integrating NFT tools into their ecosystems, giving users and creators more control over their contributions.

- **Value Beyond Transactions:** Focusing on community-building and exclusivity ensures sustained user engagement and profitability.

Redefining the Digital Economy

Big companies are reaping the benefits of Web3 by embracing decentralized data monetization models, AI-driven marketplaces, and NFT-based content ecosystems. By aligning incentives with users and creators, they are not only building new revenue streams but also redefining their roles in the digital economy.

In Web3, the power dynamic shifts from centralized entities to individuals, creating opportunities for companies to innovate, collaborate, and thrive in a user-driven, decentralized landscape. By adapting early and strategically, businesses can position themselves as leaders in this transformative era, where data and creativity are key assets that everyone has the power to own and monetize.

Index

3D asset, 41

Aave, 2, 14, 101

Adidas, 44, 48, 95, 111

Adobe, 56, 71, 85, 118

AI. See Artificial Intelligence

Amazon, 2, 62, 71, 92, 102, 111

AML. See Anti-Money
    Laundering

Andreessen Horowitz, 30

Anti-Money Laundering, 70

Apple, 63, 68, 88

Artificial Intelligence, 2, 45, 46,
    51, 52, 53, 54, 55, 56, 57, 59,
    61, 62, 63, 64, 65, 66, 75, 76,
    77, 78, 79, 80, 81, 92, 93, 97,
    98, 99, 100, 101, 102, 103,
    104, 113, 114, 115, 116, 117,
    118, 119, 120, 122, 123, 124,
    127

avatar, 39, 40, 53, 59, 61, 62, 63,
    64, 65, 66, 84

Axa, 76

Aztec, 6

BAYC. See Bored Ape Yacht
    Club

Bitcoin, 10, 13, 34

blockchain, 2, 5, 7, 8, 9, 11, 12,
    13, 17, 20, 21, 22, 24, 27, 29,
    31, 33, 34, 35, 36, 38, 39, 43,
    44, 55, 56, 60, 63, 65, 66, 68,
    69, 70, 71, 75, 77, 78, 81, 85,
    91, 92, 94, 95, 98, 100, 106,
    109, 113, 114, 117, 120, 122,
    124

BMW, 60

Bored Ape Yacht Club, 12, 110,
    126

CAGR. See Compound Annual
    Growth Rate

centralized, 1, 2, 5, 6, 7, 8, 10,
    15, 18, 19, 28, 29, 32, 41, 43,
    46, 53, 60, 67, 73, 75, 83,
    121, 127

Chainalysis, 8, 70

Chainlink, 12, 55, 100, 117

Coca-Cola, 48, 95

code is law, 11

Coinbase, 36, 76, 98

Compound Annual Growth
    Rate, 13

contract automation, 81

cryptocurrency, 2, 20, 22

cryptography, 7, 10, 17

Cryptokicks, 107

DAO. See Decentralized Autonomous Organization

DappRadar, 11, 14, 118

data integration, 81, 117

Decentraland, 26, 39, 53, 84, 94, 111, 115

decentralization, 1, 2, 9, 19, 24, 34, 38, 51, 57, 66, 98, 113, 119

Decentralized Autonomous Organization, 3, 4, 5, 19, 28, 29, 30, 32, 33, 42, 46, 54, 64, 79, 80, 94, 98, 99, 101, 104

Decentralized Finance, 5, 12, 15, 19, 20, 21, 22, 23, 24, 36, 37, 42, 51, 54, 76, 77, 110

Decentralized Identifier, 85

Decentralized Physical Infrastructure Network, 45

DeFi. See Decentralized Finance

democratic, 3

DePIN. See Decentralized Physical Infrastructure Network

DID. See Decentralized Identifier

digital identity, 10, 69, 84

digital twin, 28, 59, 60, 62, 63, 64, 65, 66

Disney, 48, 125

distributed ledger technology, 2

Epic Games, 27, 39, 52, 61, 80, 84, 92, 107, 115

ETH, 4, 13

ethical, 64, 65, 66, 73, 97, 98, 99, 101, 102, 103, 104, 108, 123

Facebook, 2, 5, 19, 38, 52, 61, 67, 69, 79, 84, 91, 111

Filecoin, 45

finance, 8, 12, 15, 24, 31, 33, 37, 51, 54, 117, 123

FT. See Fungible Token

Fungible Token, 11, 13, 15, 44, 107

Goldman Sachs, 54, 78, 81

Google, 2, 5, 19, 36, 67, 84, 99, 108, 114, 119, 122

governance, 3, 4, 5, 9, 14, 18, 28, 29, 30, 31, 32, 42, 54, 57, 64, 75, 76, 79, 80, 81, 94, 100, 101, 102, 104

Gucci, 26, 64, 92

healthcare, 8, 31, 46, 70, 86, 117, 123

IBM, 55, 65, 69, 78, 81, 86, 98, 117

Kia America, 48

Layer 1, 19, 33, 34, 35, 36, 42

Layer 2, 19, 33, 35, 36, 37, 42

Louis Vuitton, 26

MakerDAO, 4, 30, 54

Mastercard, 20, 21

Mesh, 41

Meta, 38, 52, 61, 69, 79, 81, 91, 96, 111, 116, 119, 122

metaverse, 14, 19, 25, 38, 39, 40, 41, 42, 51, 52, 60, 61, 62, 64, 65, 67, 68, 69, 70, 71, 73, 84, 91, 92, 93, 94, 95, 96, 111, 115, 125

Microsoft, 36, 41, 64, 68, 84, 93, 96, 98, 109, 116, 119

NFT. See Non-Fungible Token

Nike, 25, 48, 62, 70, 92, 96, 107, 115, 125

Non-Fungible Token, 2, 11, 12, 13, 14, 15, 16, 17, 24, 25, 26, 27, 28, 36, 40, 44, 48, 56, 64, 65, 70, 73, 85, 92, 95, 107, 108, 110, 115, 118, 122, 125, 126, 127

NVIDIA, 52

Ocean Protocol, 47, 87, 106, 122

Onyx, 20, 22

Optimistic Rollup, 35

oracle, 76, 78, 81, 100, 117

Ownership Economy, 1, 105, 126

PayPal, 22, 36, 76, 94, 114

PepsiCo, 48

personal data store, 85

Platform Economy, 1

private key, 10

Procter & Gamble, 87

Propy, 12, 27

public key, 10

RealT, 16

Reddit, 86

Roblox, 26, 92

Ronin, 35

RTFKT, 25, 48, 92

Salesforce, 86

skin in the game, 3, 16

smart contract, 7, 11, 12, 17, 23, 32, 34, 45, 55, 75, 76, 77, 81, 124, 125

Spotify, 53, 78, 85, 109

Tesla, 60

The Sandbox, 39, 94, 111, 115

token-based voting, 5

tokenization, 7, 13, 15, 16, 17, 21, 86, 105, 112

transparent, 3, 4, 5, 6, 8, 11, 12, 16, 19, 20, 23, 28, 33, 41, 43, 45, 46, 47, 64, 66, 68, 69, 71, 73, 79, 86, 87, 88, 93, 94, 96, 97, 98, 103, 108, 121 travel insurance, 45

Twitter, 2, 5

Ubisoft, 27, 56

Uniswap, 2, 5, 14, 29, 79, 101

Uniswap DAO, 5

user-owned, 3, 7, 53, 97

virtual clothing, 41

Visa, 20, 21, 36, 77, 81, 88

Walmart, 39, 64

Warner Music Group, 125

Web1, 2

Web2, 1, 5, 6, 8, 10, 15, 19, 41,
  43, 46, 59, 60, 67, 68, 69, 73,
  84, 91, 92, 105, 118, 122

Web3, 1, 2, 3, 4, 5, 6, 7, 8, 9, 10,
  12, 13, 15, 17, 19, 28, 33, 37,
  38, 41, 42, 43, 44, 45, 46, 47,
  48, 49, 51, 53, 55, 57, 59, 60,
  61, 63, 64, 65, 66, 67, 68, 70,
  71, 72, 73, 75, 76, 79, 80, 81,
  83, 84, 85, 86, 87, 88, 89, 91,
  93, 96, 97, 98, 99, 102, 103,
  104, 105, 106, 108, 111, 112,
  113, 118, 119, 120, 121, 122,
  127

xDai, 35

Zero-Knowledge Proof, 6, 70

ZKP. See Zero-Knowledge
  Proof

zkSync, 6